STAGE DESIGN
EMOTIONS

PPVMEDIEN

© 2010
PPVMEDIEN GmbH, Bergkirchen

1. Auflage 2010

ISBN 978-3-941531-68-0

© Fotos: Ralph Larmann
Redaktion & Struktur: Tabea Nagel
Produktionsmanagement: Susanne Guidera
Grafik: Kostantin Frhr. v. Gaisberg-Schöckingen
Foto Ralph Larmann: Reinhard Langschied
Druck: Westermann Druck Zwickau

Alle Rechte vorbehalten. Nachdruck, auch auszugsweise,
sowie Vervielfältigungen jeglicher Art nur mit schriftlicher
Genehmigung der PPVMEDIEN GmbH.

INHALTSVERZEICHNIS/CONTENT

VORWORT VON WILLIE WILLIAMS/	
FOREWORD BY WILLIE WILLIAMS	6
EINLEITUNG/INTRODUCTION	10

MUSICAL
Wicked – Die Hexen von Oz	14
West Side Story	34
Ich will Spaß!	46
Sorbas	56

CONCERT
U2 – 360°	66
Kylie Minogue – KYLIEX2008	94
The Police – Reunion Tour	112
Genesis – Turn it on again	126
P!nk – Funhouse	146
a-ha – Ending on a High Note	162
DJ Bobo – Fantasy	174
Die Fantastischen Vier – Fornika für Alle	186
Bon Jovi – Lost Highway	196
Tina Turner – Tina!: 50th Anniversary World Tour	210
Mario Barth – Worldrecord Show	232

OPERA
Aida	248
Tosca	260
Die Passagierin	272
Nabucco	284

TV SHOW
Eurovision Song Contest 2010	296
Sommer Wetten, dass..? 2007	308
Eurovision Song Contest 2009	314

SPECIAL EVENT
NOBEL Prize Banquet 2009	328
Mercedes-Benz Carwalk, IAA 2007	338
BOSS Black Fashion Show 2009	346
MAYDAY 2010	354
AIDAdiva – Ship of Light	368
Season of Light 2010	384

BIOGRAFIE/BIOGRAPHY RALPH LARMANN	394
KÜNSTLERVERZEICHNIS/CREDITS	396
DANK/ACKNOWLEDGEMENT	400

VORWORT VON WILLIE WILLIAMS/
FOREWORD BY WILLIE WILLIAMS
EINLEITUNG/INTRODUCTION

VORWORT

Wann immer ich mich dazu verleiten lasse, das Showbusiness als überflüssigen Luxus anzusehen, denke ich an die vielen Gelegenheiten, bei denen ein vollkommen Fremder auf mich zukam, um mir zu sagen, dass eine der Shows, an denen ich beteiligt war (vielleicht sogar eine, an die ich mich nur noch vage erinnern kann), der „Höhepunkt seines Lebens" gewesen sei. Dies erscheint vielleicht etwas übertrieben, doch eine gute musikalische Performance hat zweifellos die Kraft, mitzureißen, zu inspirieren und Spuren im Leben eines Menschen zu hinterlassen – und dies, wie es nur wenige andere Formen der Kunst vermögen.

Wer an der Produktion von Live-Shows arbeitet, für den gerät die Bühne zu einer Leinwand, doch unsere Kunst liegt in der Gestaltung von vergänglichen kollektiven Erlebnissen. Eine großartige Performance wird zu einem Austausch von Energie, der das Publikum vollkommen fesselt und ihm die ausgesprochen seltene Möglichkeit verleiht, voll und ganz in diesem einen Moment aufzugehen.

Die Einzigartigkeit dieser Macht tritt im digitalen Zeitalter immer deutlicher hervor. Trotz You Tube und 3D IMAX: Es ist unwahrscheinlich, dass die virtuelle Welt jemals in der Lage sein wird, die emotionale Wucht einer großen Menschenmenge zu vermitteln, die gemeinsam einen ganz bestimmten Moment erlebt und diese Erfahrung in Echtzeit teilt. Wir befinden uns hier eben nicht im Digital-Fernsehen mit Instant Replay, es ist die Erfahrung, die gleiche Luft zu atmen, wie ein anderer Mensch, der direkt vor deinen Augen etwas tut, was *du* nicht tun kannst.

Man wird das gewisse Etwas eines solchen Erlebnisses nie einfangen können – doch das ist ganz sicher kein Nachteil! Mir ist klar geworden, dass die Vergänglichkeit der Dinge, die wir tun, gleichzeitig ihren größten Wert darstellt. Zu wissen, dass dieses Erlebnis nur in diesem einen Augenblick ganz und gar genossen werden kann, hat eine befreiende Wirkung. Man kann diesen besonderen Augenblick nicht festhalten, man kann ihn nicht in Flaschen abfüllen oder für später konservieren. Die Konzeption jeglicher Art von Show ist ein sehr intensiver, gemeinschaftlicher Prozess, der sowohl technische und künstlerische als auch diplomatische Fähigkeiten erfordert. Designer, Manager und Hersteller sind notwendig, um den Raum für eine Performance zu schaffen – doch wir sind nicht diejenigen, die ihn nutzen werden. Unsere Aufgabe ist es, Magie für den Zuschauer zu erzeugen, während wir für den Künstler gleichzeitig eine Umgebung zur Verfügung stellen, in der er sich komplett entfalten kann. Daher gestalten wir nicht für uns selbst; wir erschaffen einen Raum, den der Künstler dominieren und sich aneignen können muss. Unsere Herausforderung ist deshalb vergleichbar damit, einen maßgeschneiderten Anzug für eine andere Person herzustellen. Aus diesem Grund beginne ich die Konzeption einer Show da-

mit, von der Perspektive des Künstlers auszugehen und die des Publikums mit einzubeziehen. Die Zauberei besteht darin, diese beiden Blickwinkel miteinander in Einklang zu bringen.

In den letzten 30 Jahren hat der technische Fortschritt den Prozess des Show-Designs vollkommen revolutioniert. Die 1980er Jahre brachten uns computergesteuerte Moving Lights, durch die anspruchsvollere Effekte erzeugt werden konnten und die völlig neue Gestaltungsmöglichkeiten eröffneten. Die 1990er Jahre führten Video-Inhalte als Ergänzung zur Kameraübertragung ein, wodurch „Close-ups" auch für Zuschauer in den letzten Reihen ermöglicht wurden. Das neue Jahrtausend brachte den Fortschritt der LED-Technologie, die mobile Videowände in zuvor unvorstellbaren Dimensionen ermöglichte.

Ich stand vielen dieser „Fortschritte" sehr skeptisch gegenüber, denn obwohl sie manchmal sehr wirkungsvolle und befreiende Instrumente sind, bewirken sie doch eine starke Tendenz zur Vereinheitlichung. Wenn man durch den Vorgänger dieses Buches blättert, ist es überraschend, das überwältigende Spektrum an Theater- und Opern-Designs zu sehen, um dann plötzlich festzustellen, dass vor einigen Jahren fast alle Konzertbühnen ein und derselben Ästhetik folgten. Video, LED & Medienserver sind den Faustischen Pakt mit dem Show-Design eingegangen. Er hatte seinen Ursprung in den Konzert-Events, während Theater, Oper und Corporate Events ihm gierig folgten.

Das vorliegende Buch ist ein Werk, in dem Großartiges festgehalten wird, aber es stellt auch eine große Herausforderung dar. Als Designer und Künstler haben wir die Pflicht, die Zuschauer zum Staunen zu bringen, sie zu inspirieren und sie aus ihrem Alltagsleben herauszulösen. Die Magie einer Show hängt nicht von ihrer Größe oder ihrem Budget ab – sie geht von den Ideen aus, die ihr zugrunde liegen – und nicht von der Materialliste! Das Streben nach Originalität und dem harmonischen Zusammenspiel aller Komponenten bedeutet manchmal harte Arbeit, doch wie einer meiner Kunden zu sagen pflegt: „Es ist leicht, Durchschnitt zu sein". Mit dieser Herausforderung vor Augen liegt meine ständige Inspirationsquelle in der Beobachtung. Wenn ich etwas Eindrucksvolles sehe, mache ich eine gedankliche Notiz davon. Dieser Eindruck bleibt dann in meinem Kopf hängen (manchmal über Jahre), bis er von einem ähnlichen Impuls befruchtet wird. Dies kann eine ganze Weile dauern und erfahrungsgemäß braucht es seine Zeit, bis daraus greifbare Ideen werden. Wenn ich eine gute Idee pro Jahr habe, bin ich damit sehr zufrieden.

Auf einer mehr praktisch orientierten Ebene versuche ich, bei der Umsetzung eines Konzepts menschliche Akzente in jede kreative Arbeit mit einzubringen. Dies wird bei den großen, technikbasierten Shows immer wichtiger. Technik alleine kann sehr kalt und unpersönlich wirken, wohingegen ausgefallene Lo-Fi-Elemente eigene Akzente setzen und mehr Begeisterung erzeugen. Es spricht nichts dagegen, den Kitzel einer Show mit visuellen Effekten zu erzeugen, doch es erfüllt mich mit viel mehr Zufriedenheit, wenn ich die Zuschauer mit menschlicher Wärme überraschen kann.

Wie bereits gesagt, ist Show-Design eine flüchtige Kunstform. Eine DVD oder Aufzeichnung der Show ist ein ganz anderes Medium, das besser dazu geeignet ist, den Ablauf eines Events festzuhalten als das Erlebnis zu vermitteln, dort gewesen zu sein. Vielleicht ist das der Grund, warum die Fotografie die angemessenere Form der Dokumentation einer Live-Show darstellt.

Ralph Larmann besitzt die bemerkenswerte Fähigkeit, das Vergängliche durch die Kunst des Stilllebens zu bannen. Viele der in diesem Buch vorgestellten Bühnen repräsentieren das Beste, was das Show-Design der Gegenwart hervorgebracht hat. Aber erst durch Ralphs technische Kunstfertigkeit und seine begnadete Fotografie verwandeln sie sich in eigenständige Kunstwerke.

Für mich persönlich ist es ein großes Privileg, in diesem Buch vertreten sein zu dürfen.

Willie Williams, September 2010

FOREWORD

In uncertain times, it might be easy to view "show business" as a trivial luxury. If I am ever tempted to feel this way, I remind myself of the many occasions on which I have been approached by a complete stranger wanting to tell me that some show I was involved with (maybe even one that I only vaguely remember) was "the high point of their life." This may be overstating the case, but it is certainly true that when music-based live performance fulfills its potential, it has a power to transport, to inspire and to punctuate people's lives in a way that very few other art forms can.

For those of us who work in the production of live shows, the stage is our canvas but our art lies in the creation of transitory, communal events. A great performance becomes an exchange of energy that absorbs its audience, affording them the increasingly rare sense of being completely in the moment.

The uniqueness of this power is becoming more apparent in the digital age. From You Tube to 3D IMAX, it is unlikely that the virtual world will ever be able to replicate the emotional impact of a large group of people gathering together in a single place at a particular moment, to share a communal experience in real time. This isn't digital TV with instant replay, it is the experience of being in the same airspace as another human being who is doing something that you can't do, right before your eyes.

This is a phenomenon that can never truly be captured or recorded, but far from being a disadvantage, I've come to see the temporary nature of what we do as providing its greatest value. There is a liberating extravagance in knowing that this experience must be fully enjoyed right at this moment. It is not something that can be held on to, or be bottled and saved for later.

The creation of any kind of show is an intensely collaborative process, requiring skills technical, artistic and diplomatic. Designers, directors and fabricators are essential in creating the performance environment, but we are not the people who will use it. Our task is to create magic for the viewer whilst providing a space where the performer can flourish.

In this sense we are not creating for ourselves; we are building an environment that the performers must be able to dominate and make their own. It is an undertaking very much like that of making a suit of clothes for someone else to wear. Consequently, in designing a show I begin by considering the perspective of the performer and also that of the audience. The weaving together of these two viewpoints is where the alchemy lies.

Over the past 30 years, technology has utterly revolutionized the process of show design. The 1980s brought computerised moving lights, capable of creating vastly more sophisticated effects and opening up entirely new design opportunities. The 1990s introduced "video content" as a supplement to camera coverage bringing close ups to the people in the far seats. The 2000s brought the rise of L.E.D. technology, permitting portable video screens of a previously unimaginable scale.

Many of these "advances" I have been very sceptical about because, although occasionally powerful and liberating tools, they have had a powerful tendency to homogenise. It is startling to look through Stage Design volume 1, to see the vast range of theatre & opera designs and then to note the extent to which almost all the concert touring stages seem to share a single aesthetic. Video, LED & media servers have become the great Faustian pact of show design, initially in concert touring but with theatre, opera & corporate events all keen to follow suit.

This book is a document, a record of greatness, but it also serves as a challenge. As designers, as artists we have a duty to amaze, to inspire and to bring viewers out of their everyday lives. Regardless of scale or budget, the magic of a show resides in its ideas, not in its equipment lists. Striving for originality and connection can be hard work at times but, as one particular client of mine is fond of saying, "It's easy to be average." Faced with this challenge, my most consistent source of inspiration has been the act of observation. If I see something that has an atmosphere I like, I'll make a mental note of it. It might then sit in my head (sometimes for years) until it cross-pollinates with something with a similar resonance. It can take a while though, and tangible ideas tend to come to me slowly. If I end up with one good idea a year, I feel like I am doing well.

On a more practical level, I always strive to bring a human, handmade element to any creative work. This becomes all the more important with large-scale, technology-based shows. Technology alone can become very cold and impersonal, whereas eccentric, lo-fi elements bring personality and joy. It is no bad thing to thrill with eye-candy, but it is greatly more satisfying to surprise the viewer with humanity and warmth.

As noted above, show design is a fleeting and transient art form. A DVD or recording of a show is a very different medium, more suited to capturing the form of an event, rather than the experience of being there. Perhaps this is what makes stills photography a more appropriate form of documentation for a live show. Through his mastery of the still image, Ralph Larmann has a remarkable ability to capture the temporal. Many of the stages pictured here present the very best face of contemporary show design, but through Ralph's original techniques and inspired use of lenses, these stages are transformed into works of art in their own right. It is a great privilege to be included amongst them.

Willie Williams, September 2010

EINLEITUNG

Nachdem ich im Jahr 2007 mit „STAGE DESIGN" meinen ersten Bildband über Top-Bühnendesigns veröffentlicht hatte, wurde mir durch die vielen positiven Resonanzen deutlich, dass ich dieses ungemein spannende Thema weiter verfolgen will und muss. Zu viele faszinierende Produktionen verschwinden mit ihren unzähligen aufwändigen Details nach ihrer Inszenierung für immer. Und meist werden sie in ihrer Ganzheit nicht oder nur unangemessen dokumentiert.

Dabei beziehe ich den Begriff „Bühne" nicht nur auf die klassische Konzert-, Opern- oder Musicalbühne. Orte unterschiedlichster Art können durch ihre Inszenierung zur Bühne werden, so auch einzelne Bauwerke oder ein Kreuzfahrtschiff. Zudem ist es meine tiefste Überzeugung, dass die Fotografie die kraftvollste Form ist, Bühnen und deren Inszenierungen für die Ewigkeit festzuhalten und visuell emotional aufgeladen zu transportieren.

So beschäftige ich mich damit, wie ich meinerseits noch mehr dazu beitragen kann, Bühnenmomente noch packender in Fotografien festzuhalten. Wenn ich im Londoner Wembley Stadium vor rund 90.000 Menschen mit der Band U2 auf der Bühne stehe, um ein 360°-Kugelpanoramafoto in den gut 30 Sekunden zu erstellen, in denen das Stadion einzig und allein komplett in Weisslicht ausgeleuchtet ist, verlangt das von mir absolute Fokussierung auf dieses sehr kleine Zeitfenster. Fünf perfekte Aufnahmen müssen für ein großes Ganzes in diesem einen Augenblick entstehen! Dabei hilft mir keine Automatik, denn alles an der Kamera und am Objektiv wird manuell justiert. Nur die Erfahrung, die ich während der Aufnahmen der Jahre zuvor gewonnen habe, hilft mir an dieser Stelle, 100 Prozent konzentriert zu sein. Und das in dieser emotional extrem, wenn auch positiv, aufgeladenen Atmosphäre des Songs „Where the streets have no name". Ich liebe meine Arbeit!

So traf ich auf viele offene Ohren für mein Anliegen, nationale und internationale Produktionen als Fotograf zu begleiten, um sie in STAGE DESIGN EMOTIONS zu veröffentlichen. Zugleich hatte ich das große Vergnügen, für einige Produktionen als Fotograf gebucht zu sein. Somit danke ich an dieser Stelle allen Menschen von ganzem Herzen, die mir ihr Vertrauen schenkten und mich in meiner Arbeit für das vorliegende Werk unterstützt haben.

Wer übrigens mehr Details zum überwiegenden Teil der hier gezeigten Produktionen erfahren will, dem sei ein Besuch der Website www.stagedesignemotions.com empfohlen. Hier finden Sie sämtliche verfügbaren Detailinformationen, Geschichten und Interviews redaktionell aufgearbeitet. Dazu kommen Links zu den Internetauftritten der beteiligten Designer und Unternehmen. Eine, wie ich meine, optimale, zeitgemäße und zugleich fortwährend erweiterbare Informationsquelle für alle, die mehr über die faszinierende Welt der Bühnen erfahren möchten. Übrigens finden Sie dort auch noch einige 360°-Kugelpanoramaaufnahmen, die sich nur mittels Webbrowser betrachten lassen.

Ralph Larmann, 1. Oktober 2010

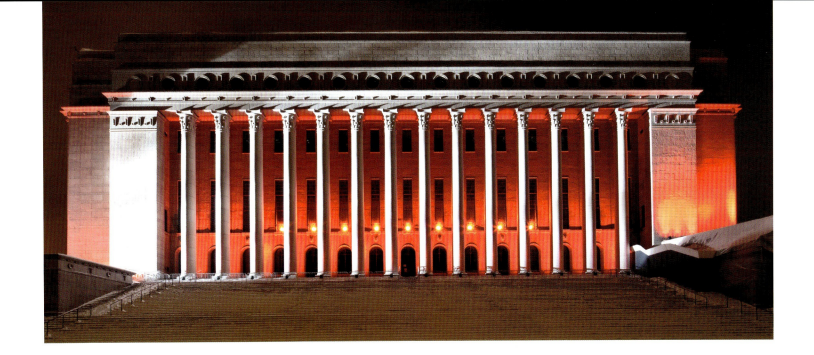

INTRODUCTION

After my first illustrated book "STAGE DESIGN" was published in 2007 the positive feedback made it all too obvious that the enthralling topic of top stage designs was something that I not only wanted to come back to but, indeed, just had to continue with. Too many fascinating projects along with the elaborate work that has been put into them just disappear once the production is finished - and usually there is either an incomplete or an inadequate record of them.

In discussing "the stage" here we are not just talking about the stage as we normally envisage it when watching concerts, operas or musicals. Very different types of places can be turned into a stage – even individual buildings or a cruise liner. Moreover, in my opinion, photography is the most powerful medium for capturing the stage and the staging, the scene and its orchestration, while conveying a visual and an emotional record of the event that will keep in eternity.

It is this aspiration to capture and to convey that has led me to embark on a quest in which I am forever trying to meet the challenge of how best I might record a particular scene, an individual moment, a fascinating event, through a photograph that is just as enthralling, just as absorbing and just as haunting as the situation itself. For instance there I am in London's Wembley Stadium on the stage with U2 in front of 90,000 and then for just some thirty seconds a "window" opens during which the stadium is completely covered in white light. Then I totally have to focus myself on this particular moment to create a 360-degree panoramic photo. Five perfect photos are required and there is no automatic mode to help me here. No, the camera and the objective are adjusted manually! It is only the years of experience that help to concentrate one hundred percent while a crescendo of noise and emotion provide this intense atmosphere - and then there is the song "Where the streets have no name". Yes, I love this job!

That is probably why numerous national and international productions have responded positively when I have asked to accompany them to photograph their productions and later have the photographs from their events published in STAGE DESIGN EMOTIONS. Indeed, I am also fortunate to have been employed as the main photographer on a number of productions, and that is why I would really like to take this opportunity not only to thank all of those who have shown confidence in me in the past but also those who are supporting this current project. Finally, for those who would like more details on the majority of the productions shown in the book, it might be a good idea for you to visit the website – www.stagedesignemotions.com - where you will find not only an array of detailed information but also background stories and interviews that have been processed by the editor. Additionally, there are also links to the websites belonging to the various designers and companies who have participated in this project and these, I think, provide not only an optimal and up-to-date source of information for anyone who wants to know more about the fascinating world of the stage, but also a source of information which can be accessed time and time again. Oh, and by the way, you will also find some 360° panoramas there which are only to be looked at using a browser.

Ralph Larmann, October, 1st 2010

MUSICAL

Wicked – Die Hexen von Oz
Palladium Theater Stuttgart
Germany | 2007

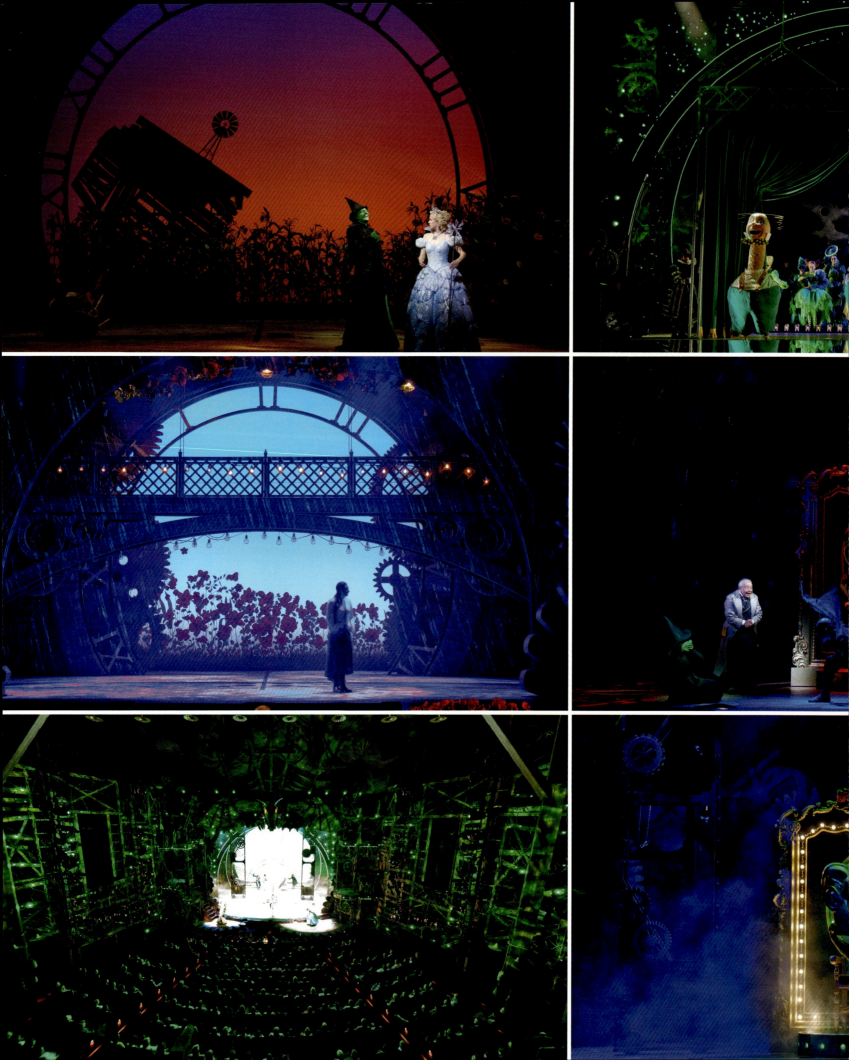

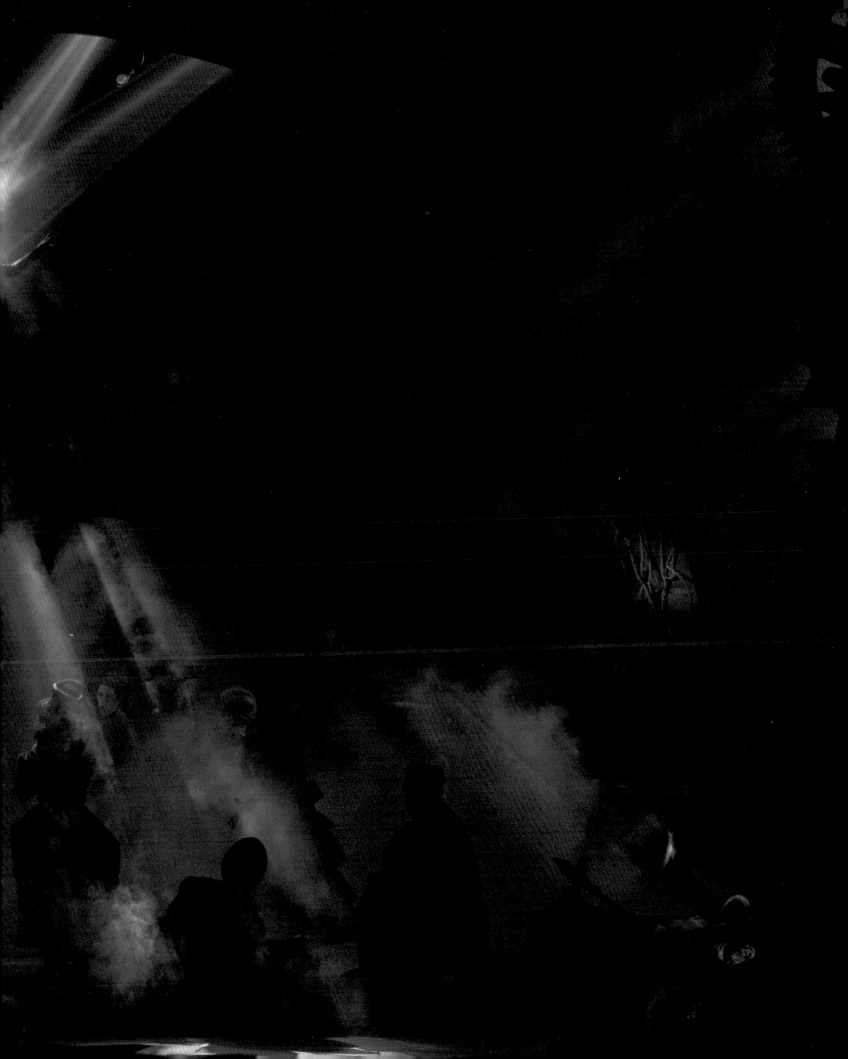

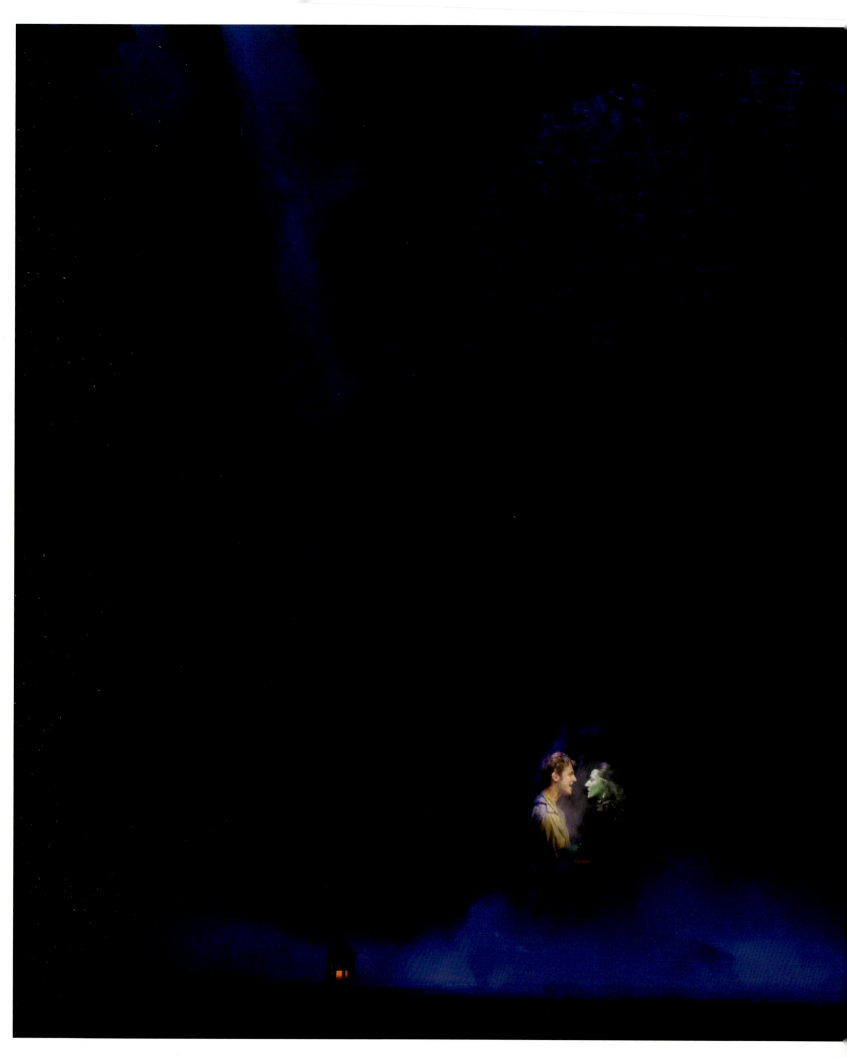

West Side Story
Rhein-Main-Theater
Niedernhausen
Germany | 2008

37

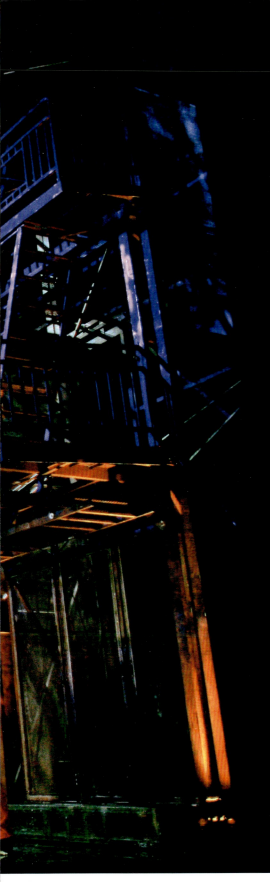

43

Ich will Spaß!
Collosseum Theater Essen
Germany | 2009

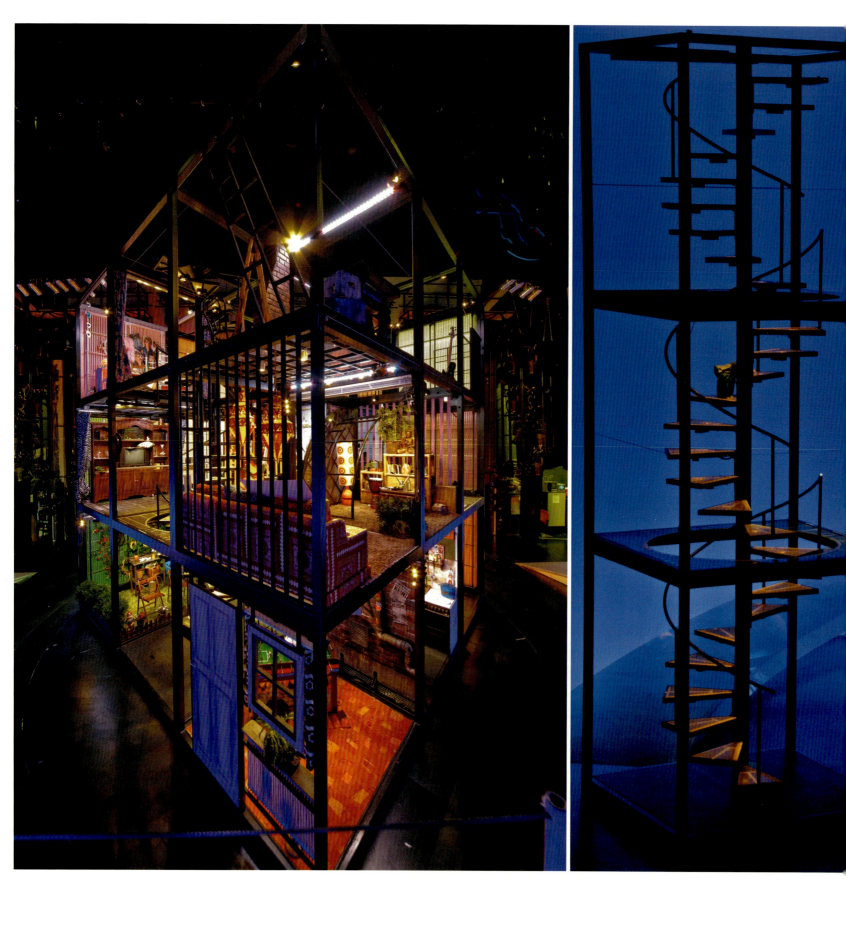

53

Sorbas
Freilichtbühne Castle Festival
Mecklenburgisches Staatstheater Schwerin
Germany | 2009

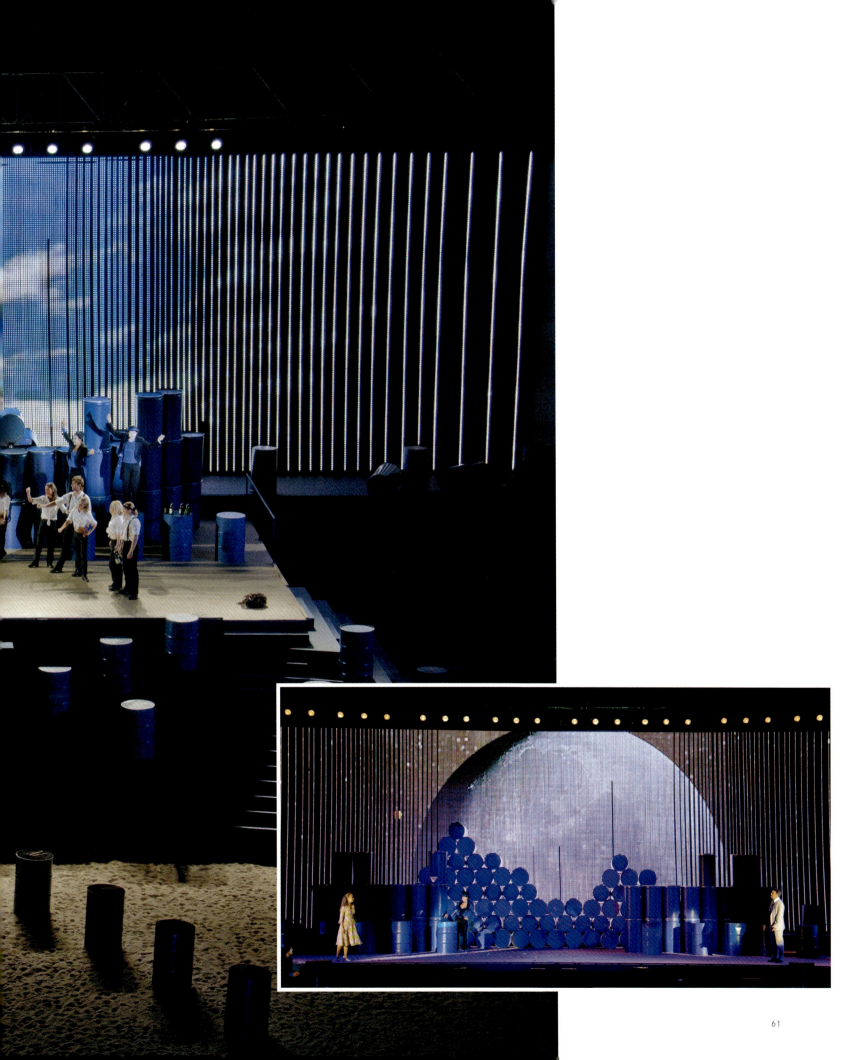

CONCERT

U2
360°
Olympic Stadium Berlin
Germany | 2009
Veltins-Arena Gelsenkirchen
Germany | 2009
Wembley Stadium London
UK | 2009

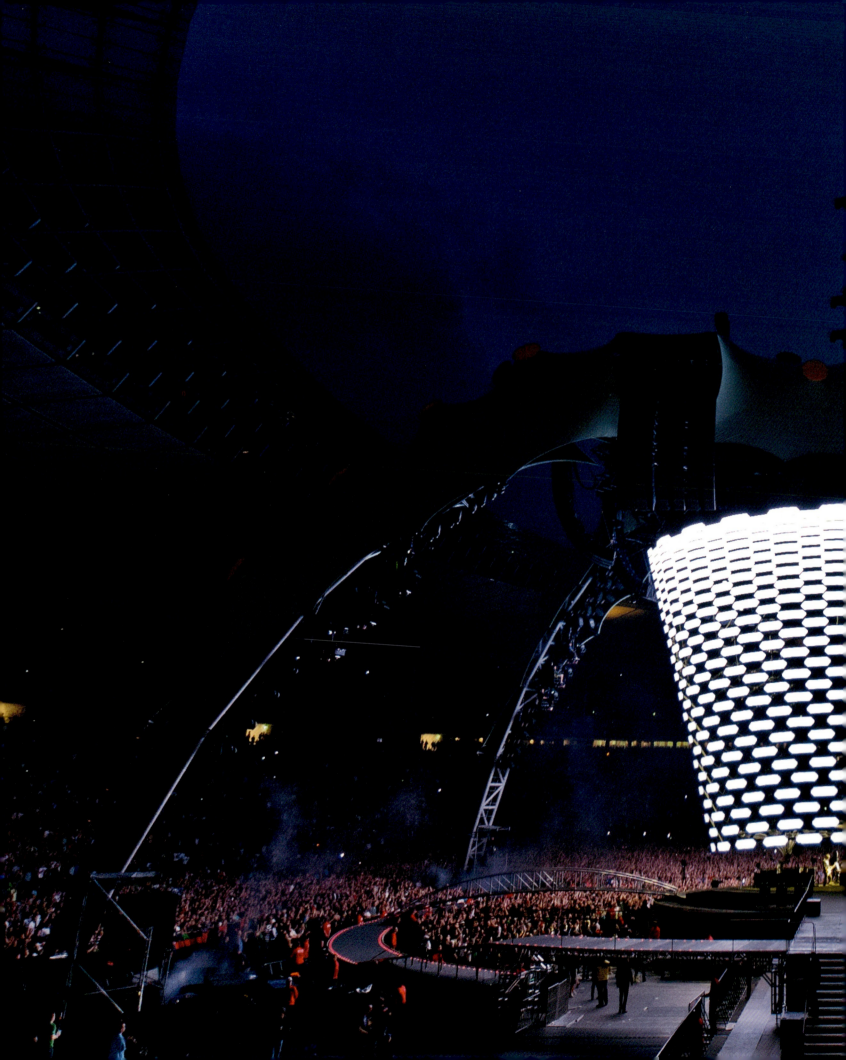

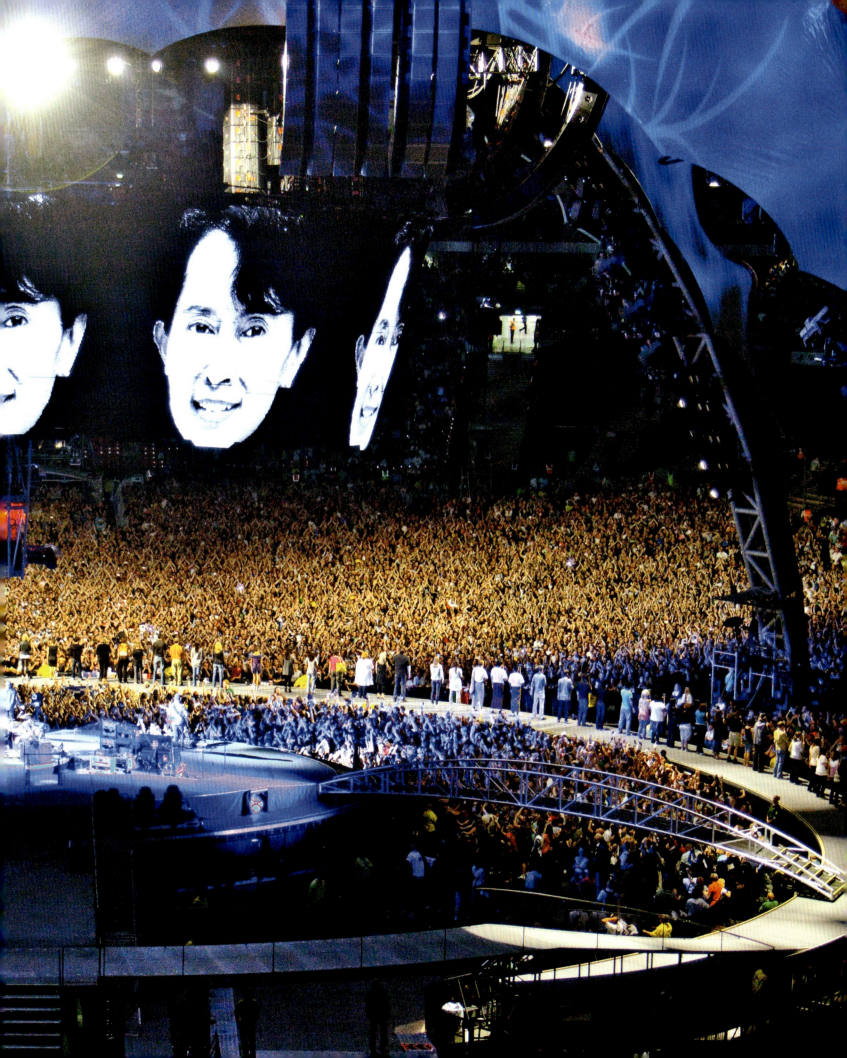

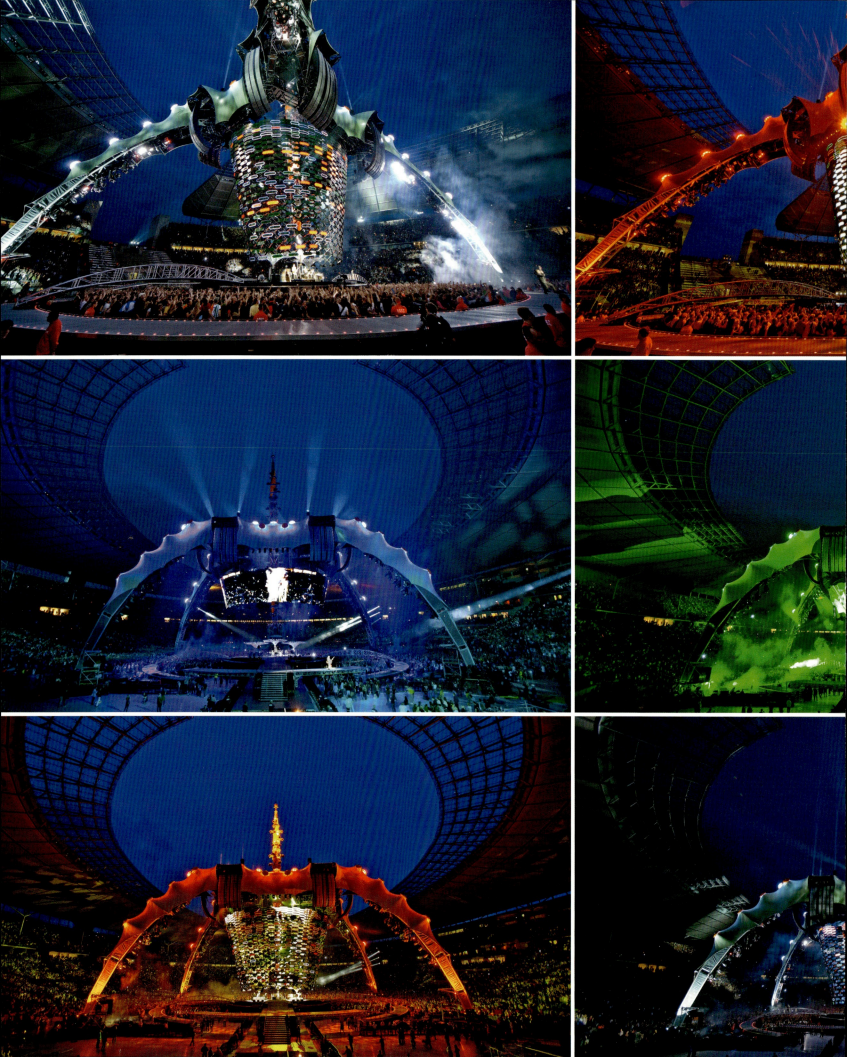

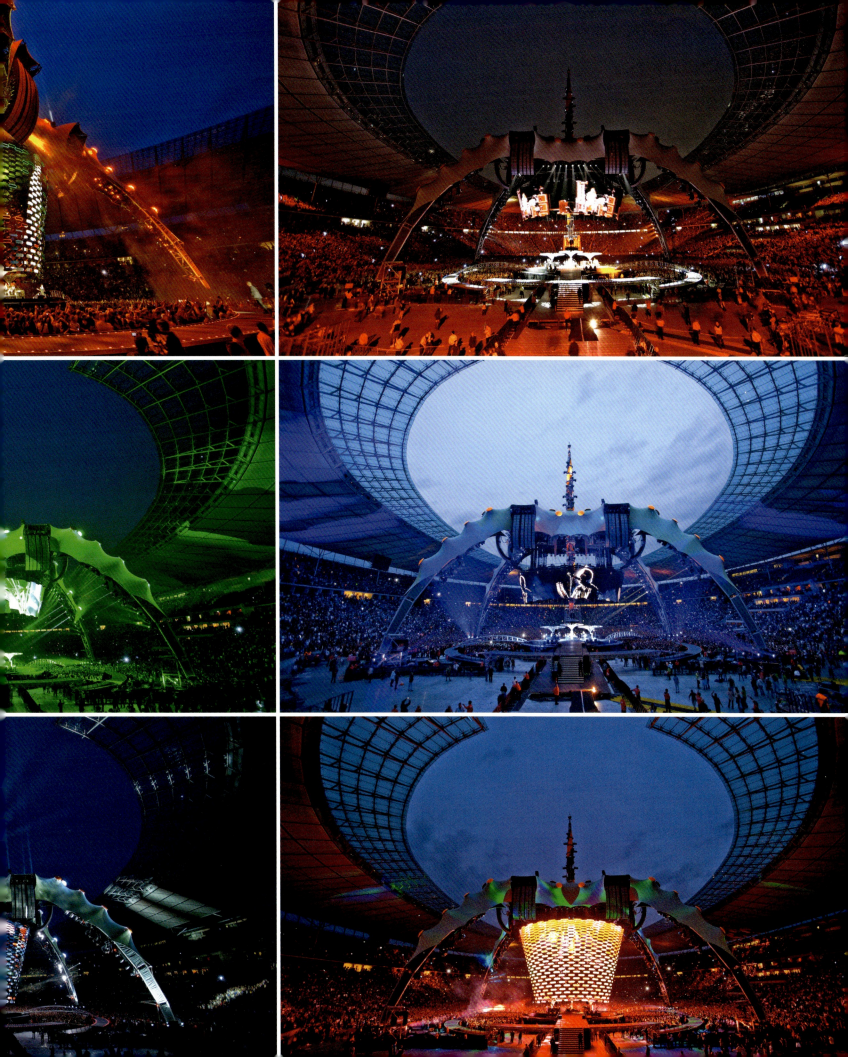

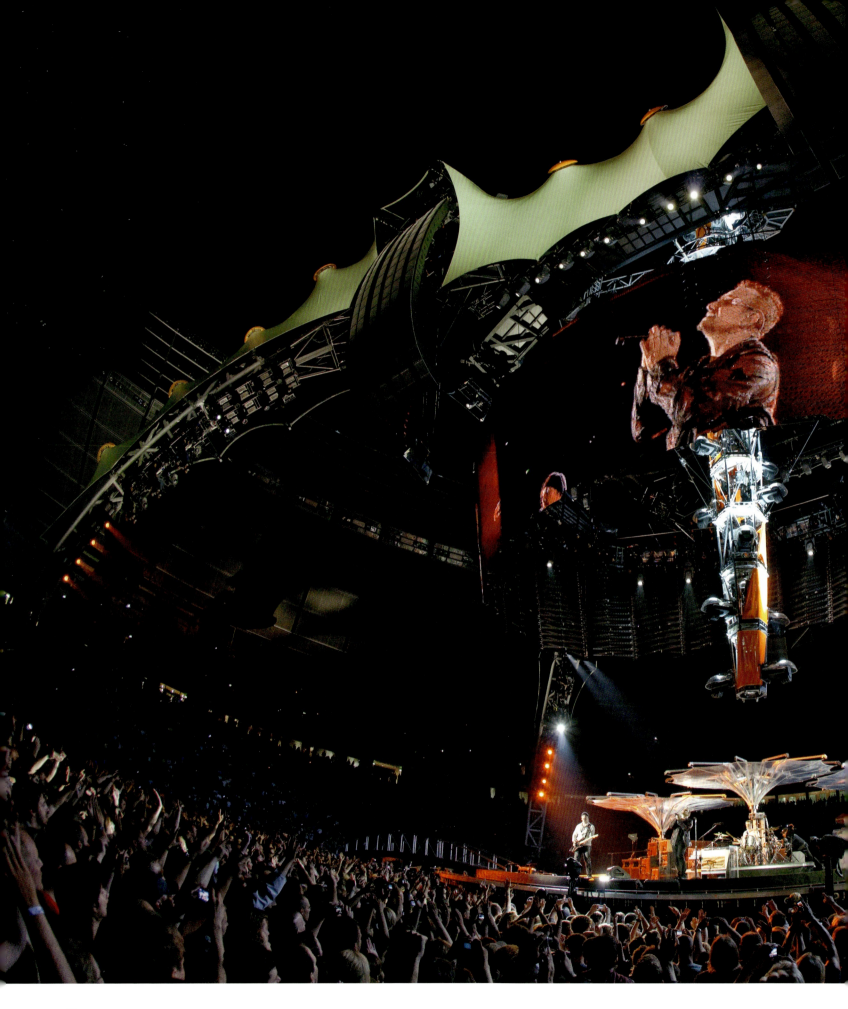

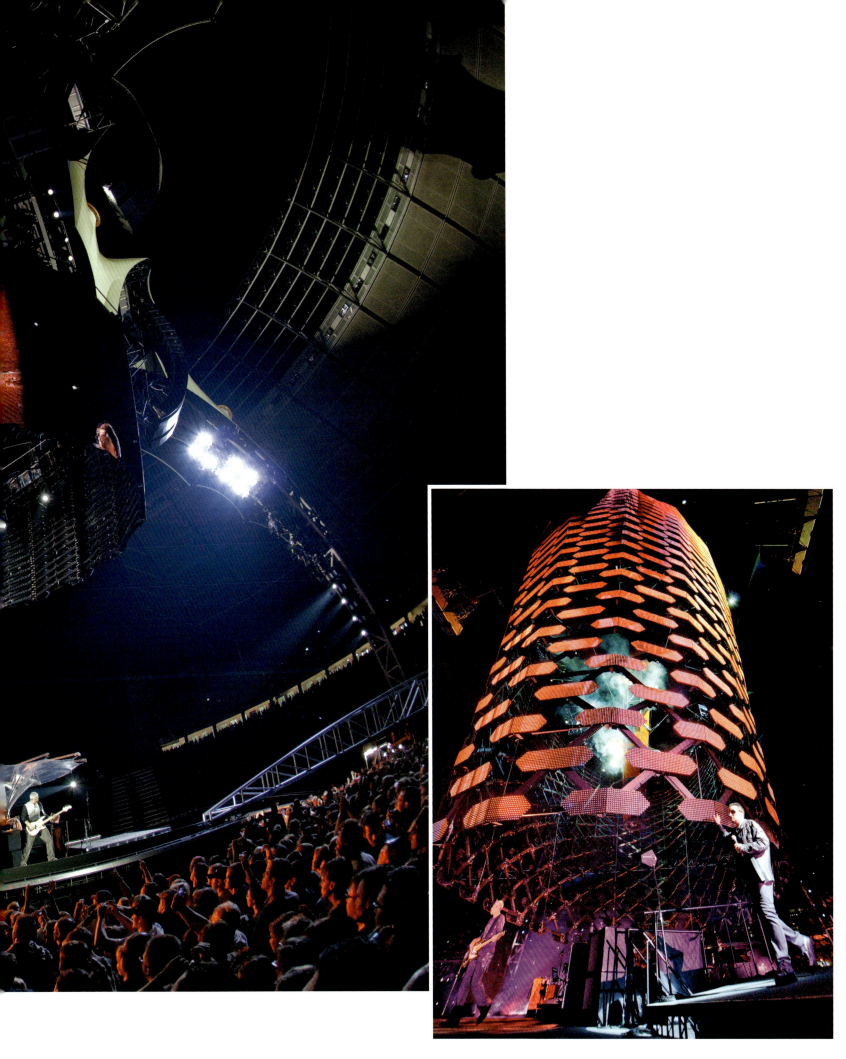

Kylie Minogue
KYLIEX2008
O2 Arena London
UK | 2008

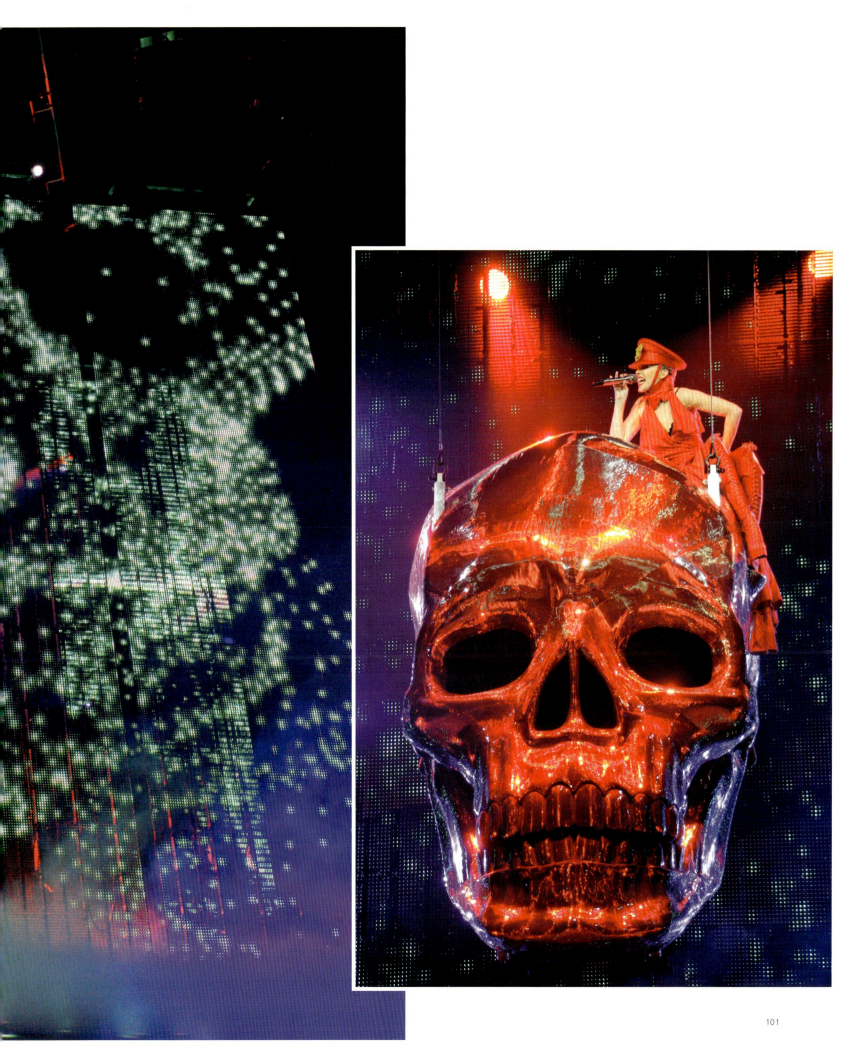

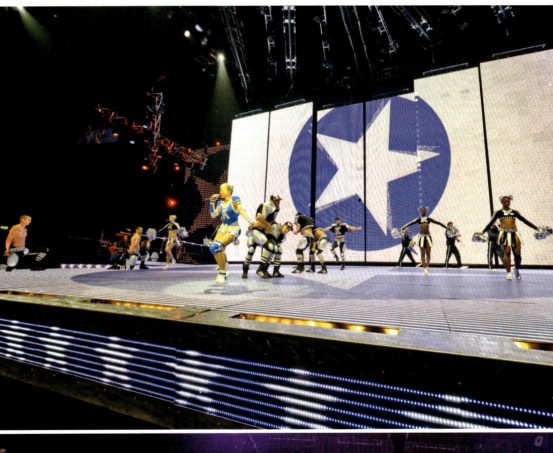

The Police
Reunion Tour
American Airlines Center Dallas
USA | 2007

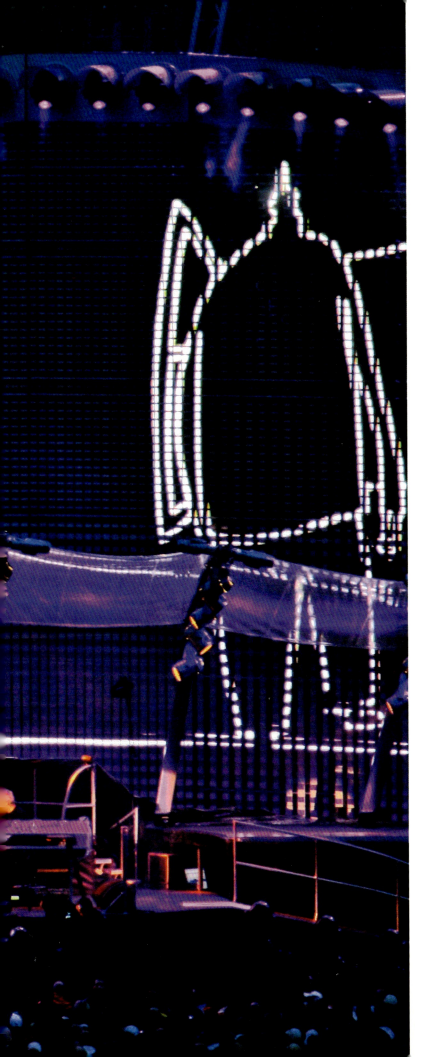

Genesis
Turn it on again
Olympic Stadium Munich
Germany | 2007

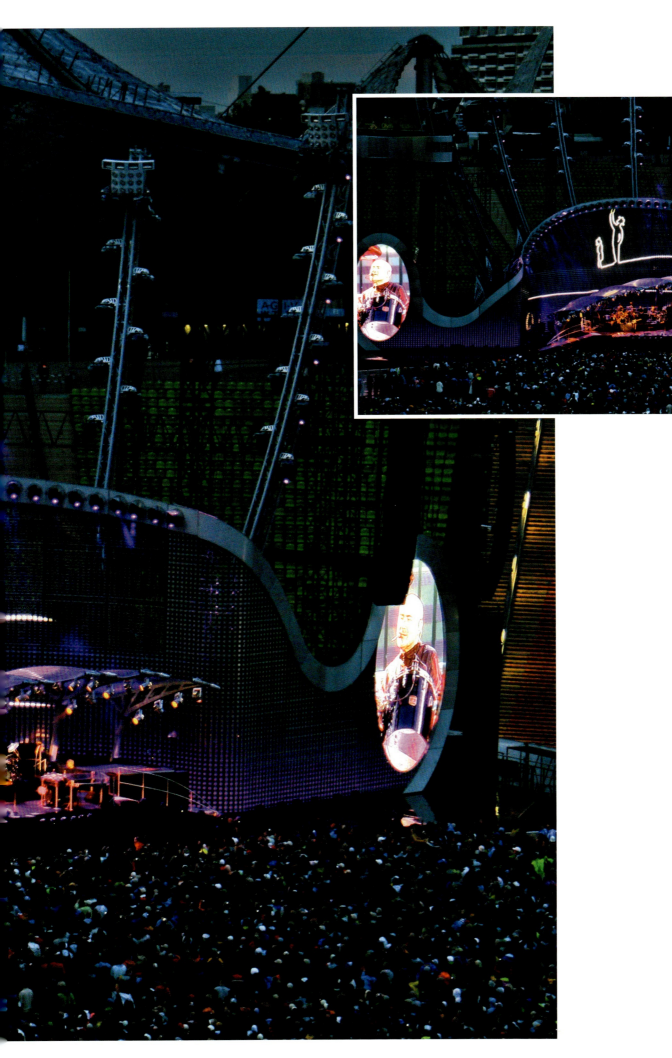

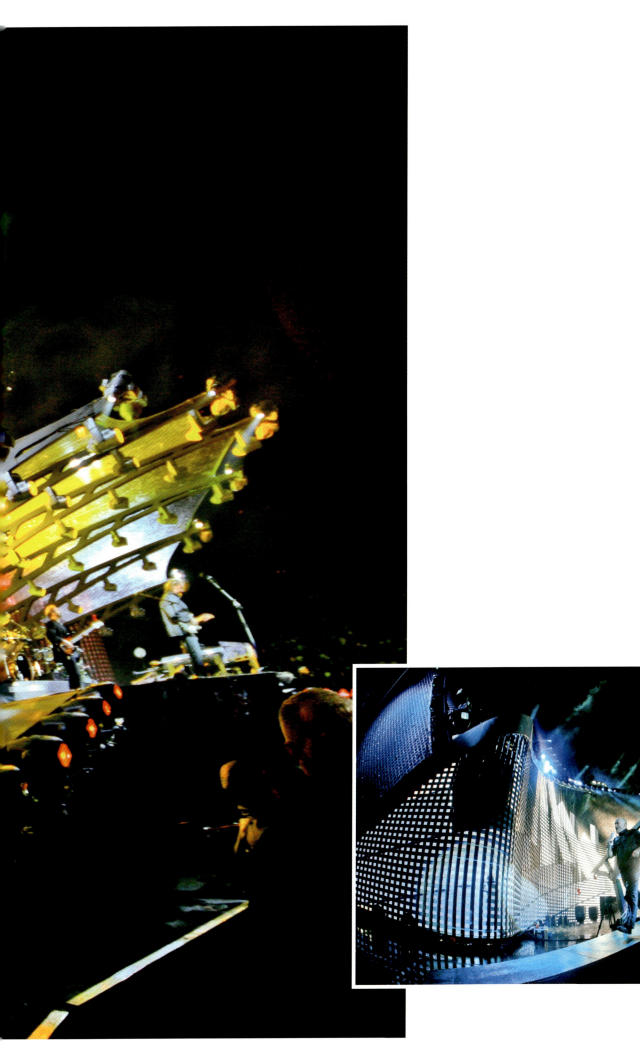

P!nk
Funhouse
SAP ARENA Mannheim
Germany | 2009

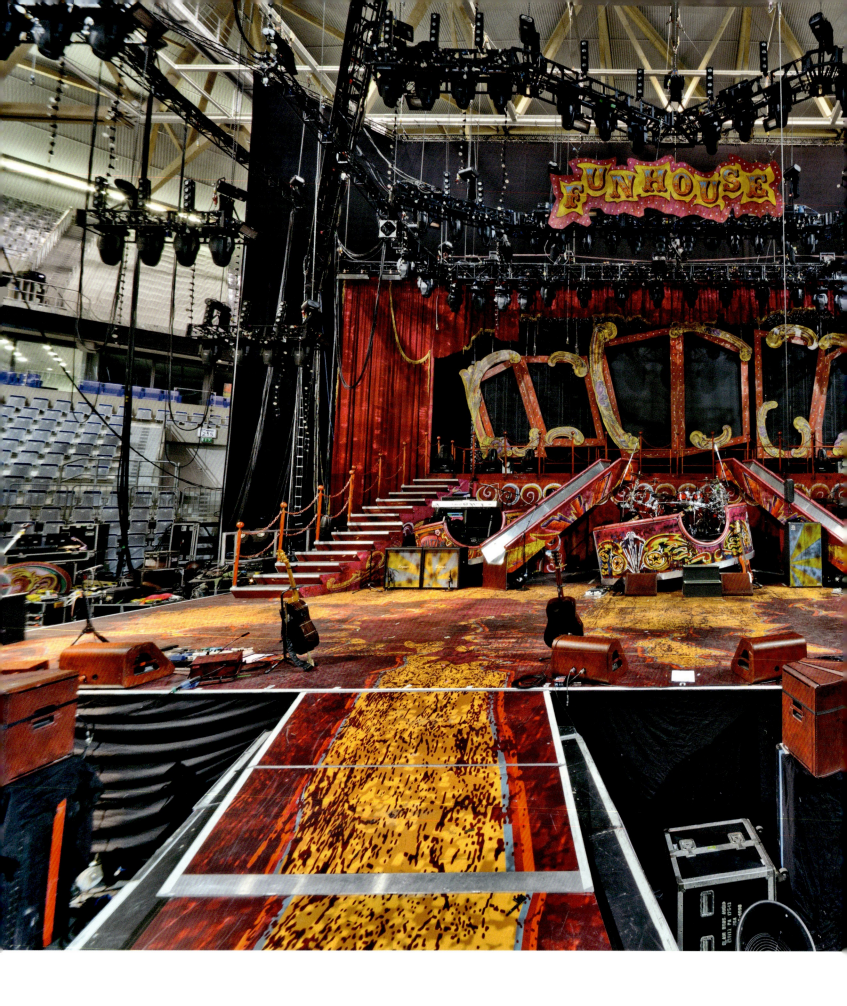

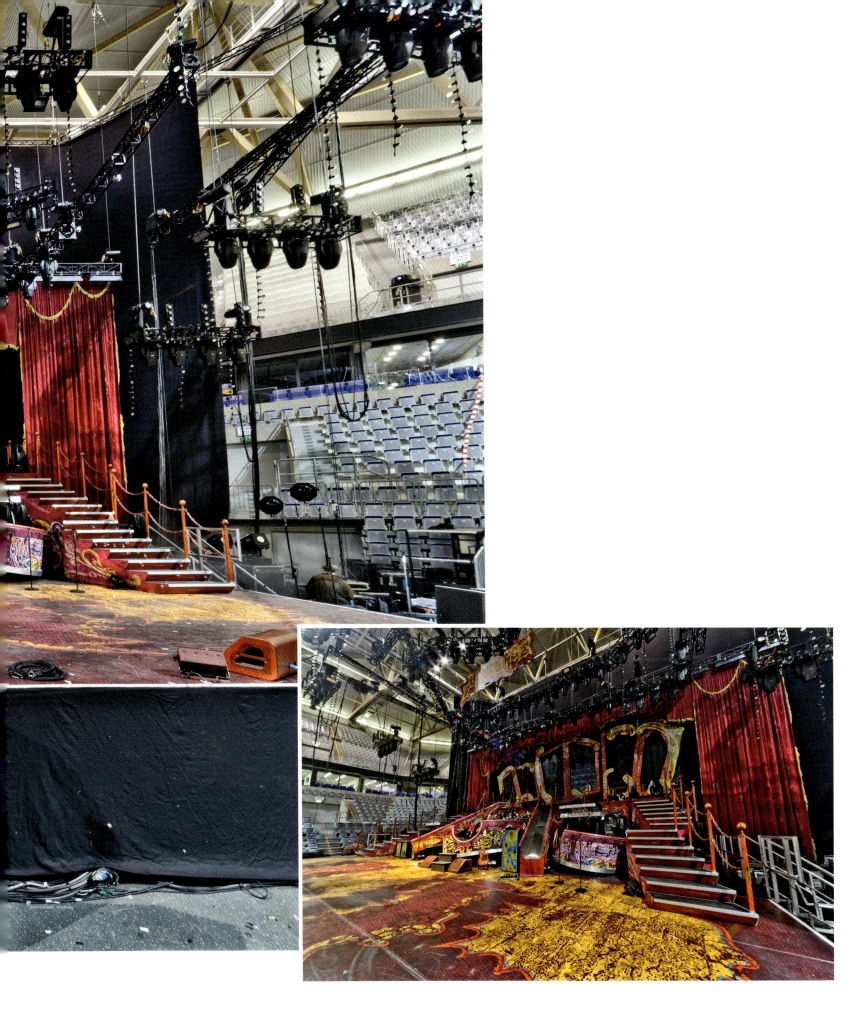

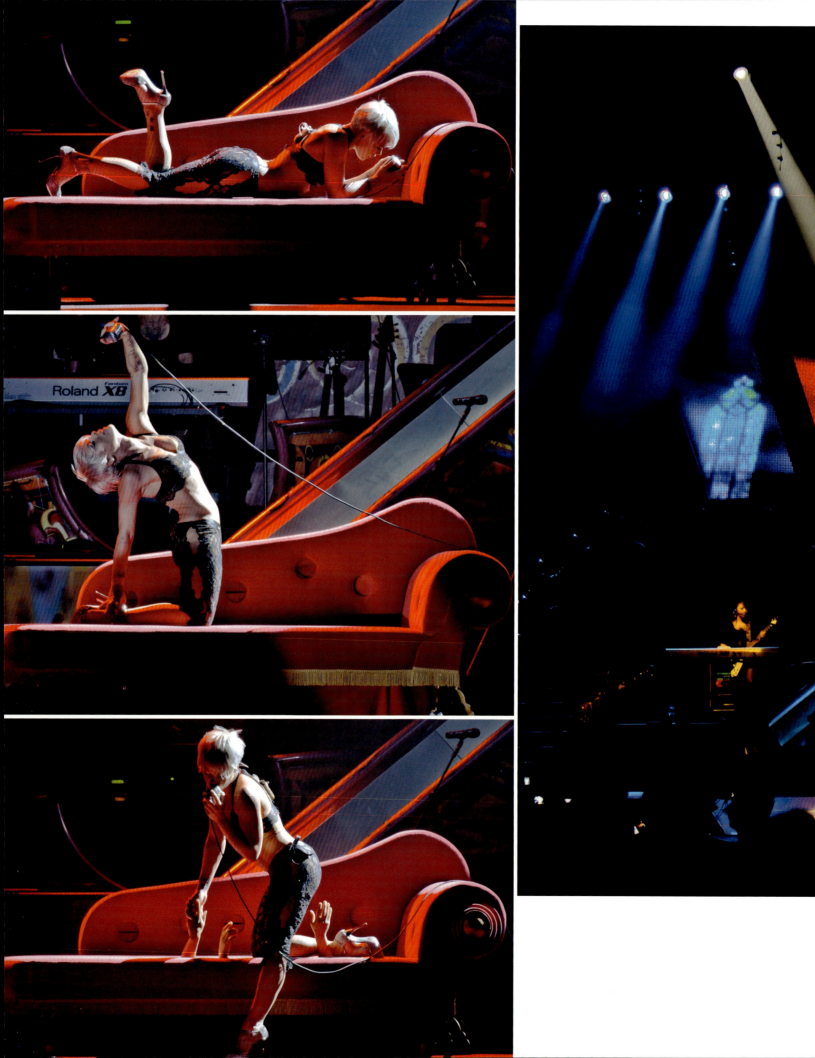

a-ha
Ending on a High Note
Sør Arena Kristiansand
Norway | 2010

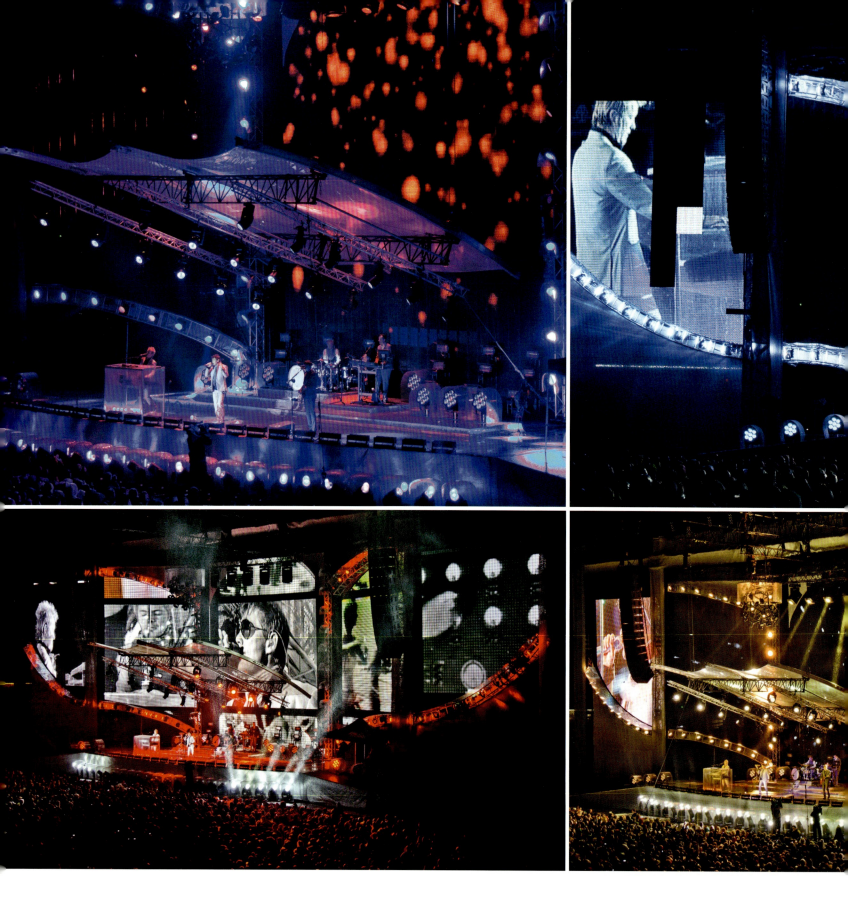

DJ Bobo
Fantasy
Lanxess-Arena Cologne
Germany | 2010

181

Die Fantastischen Vier
Fornika für Alle
Lanxess-Arena Cologne
Germany | 2007

Bon Jovi
Lost Highway
Commerzbank-Arena Frankfurt
Germany | 2008

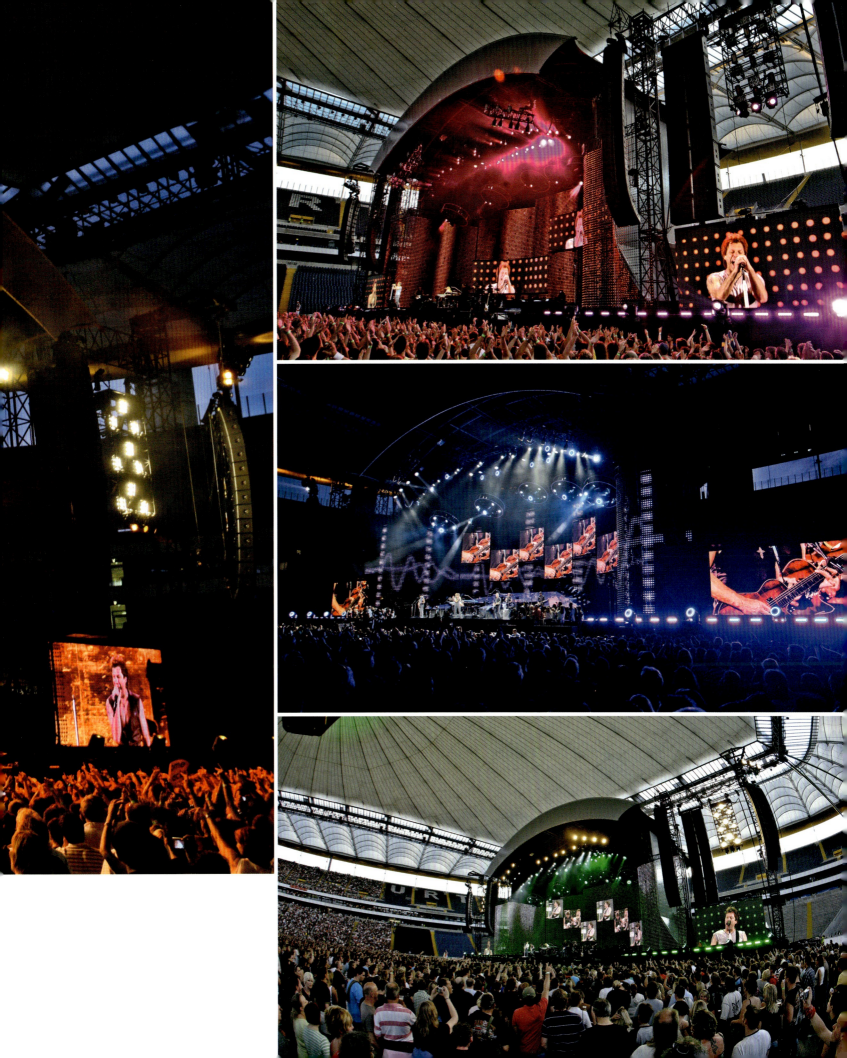

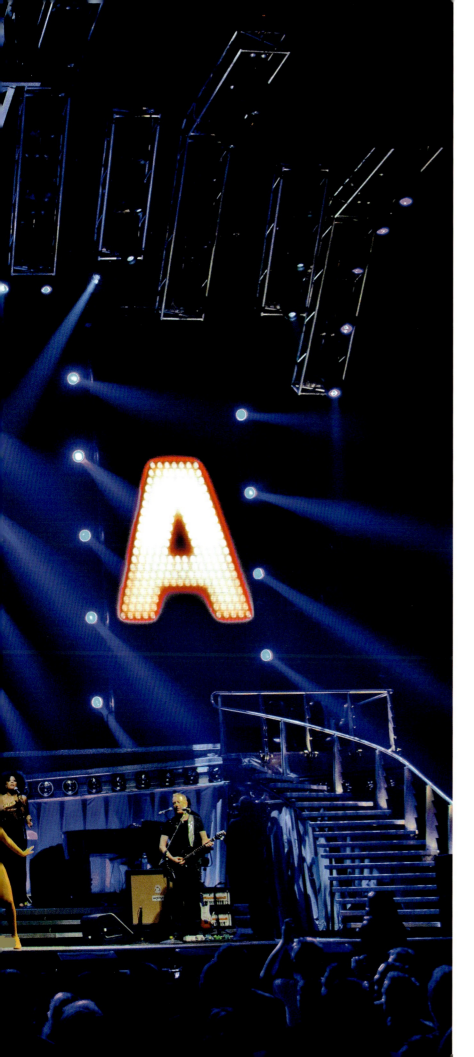

Tina Turner
Tina!: 50th Anniversary World Tour
SAP ARENA Mannheim
Germany | 2009

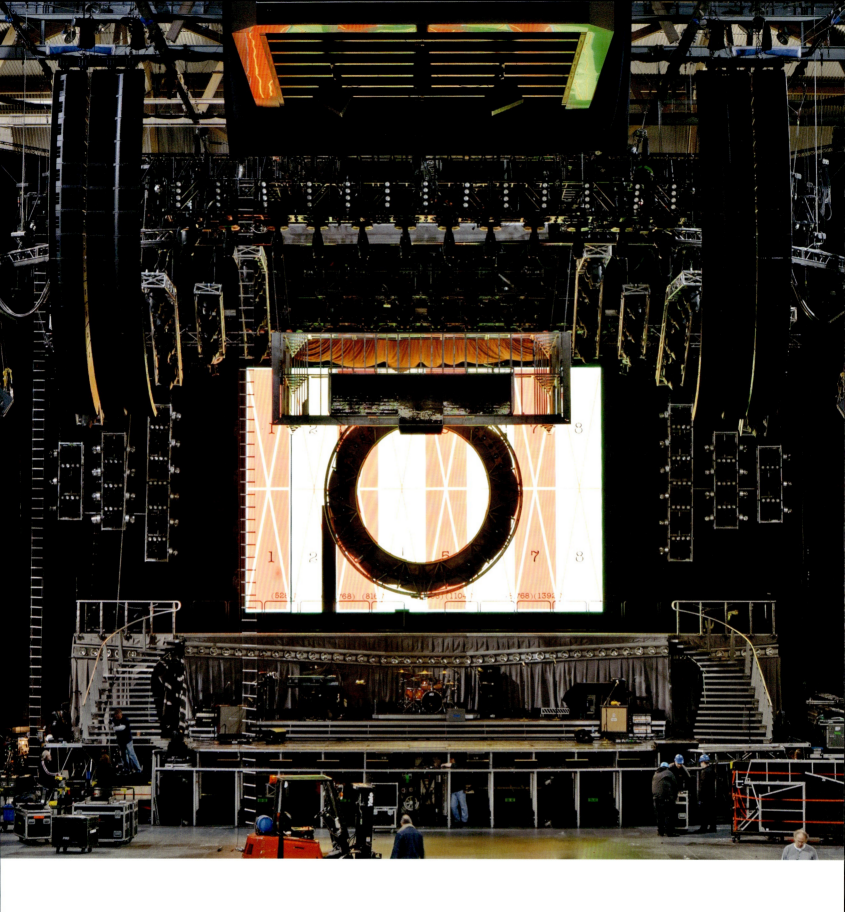

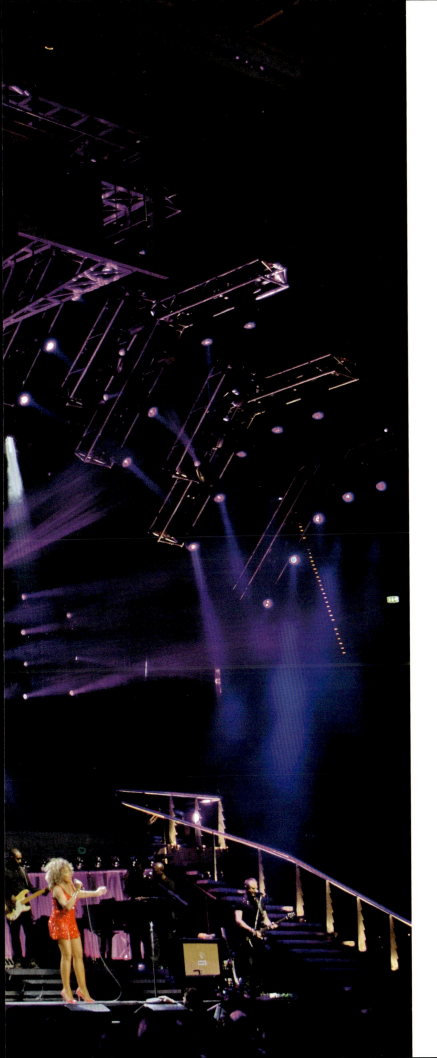

Mario Barth Worldrecord Show
Olympic Stadium Berlin
Germany | 2008

OPERA

Aida
Water Stage Bregenz
Austria | 2010

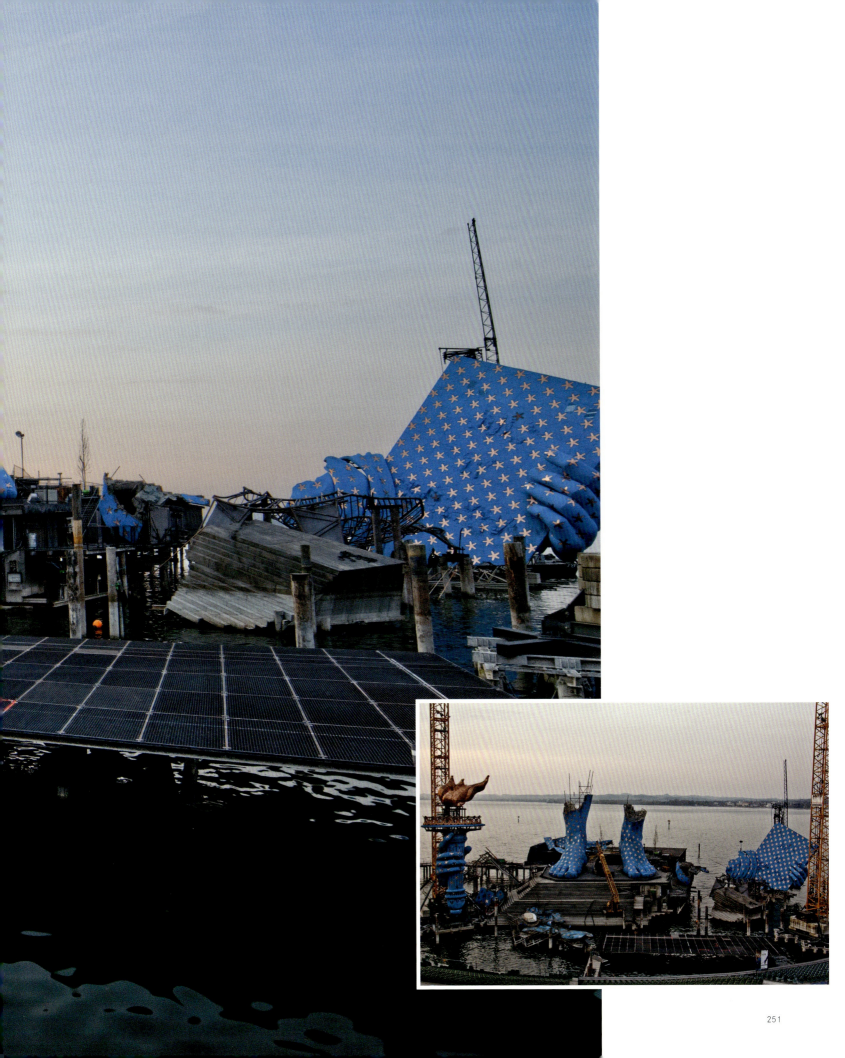

Tosca
Water Stage Bregenz
Austria | 2007

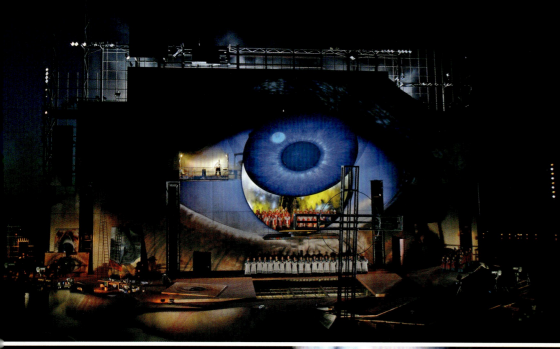
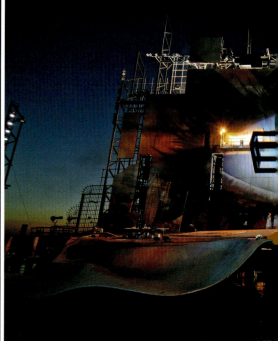

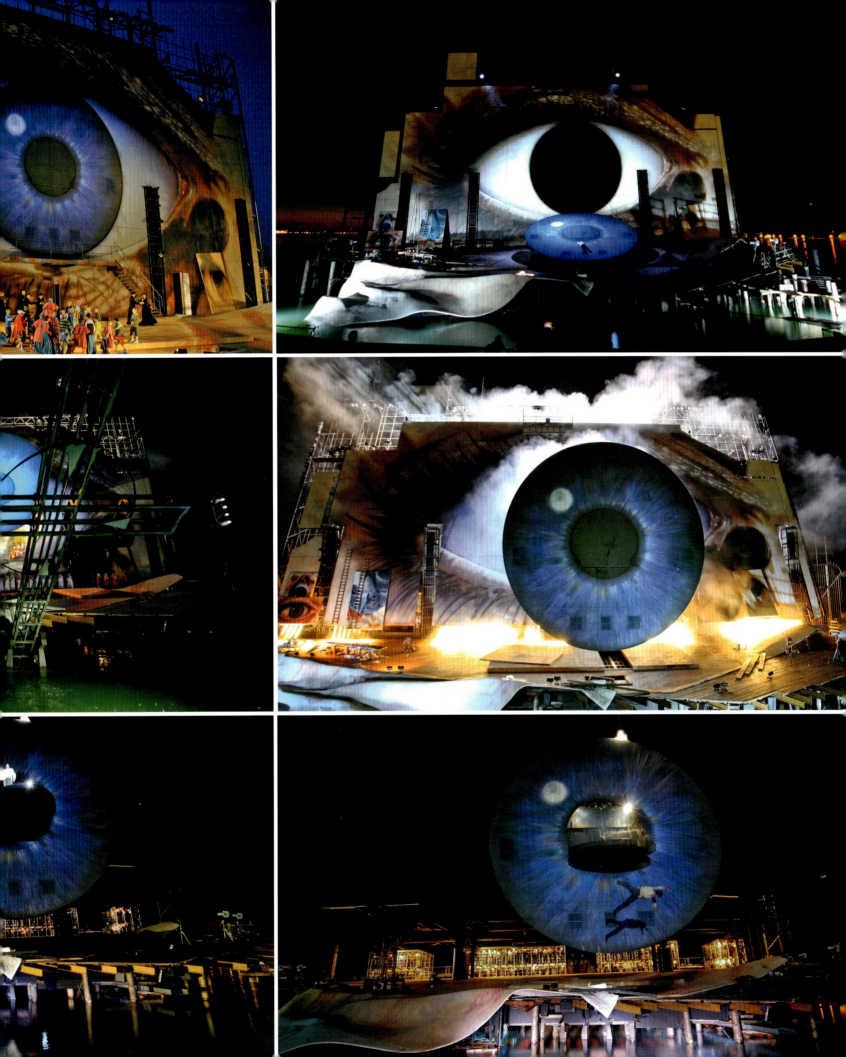

Die Passagierin
Festspielhaus Bregenz
Austria | 2010

Nabucco
Stade de France Paris
France | 2008

TV-SHOW

Eurovision Song Contest 2010
Telenor Arena Oslo
Norway | 2010

Sommer Wetten, dass..? 2007
Coliseo Balear Palma de Mallorca
Spain | 2007

Eurovision Song Contest 2009
Olimpijski-Arena Moscow
Russia | 2009

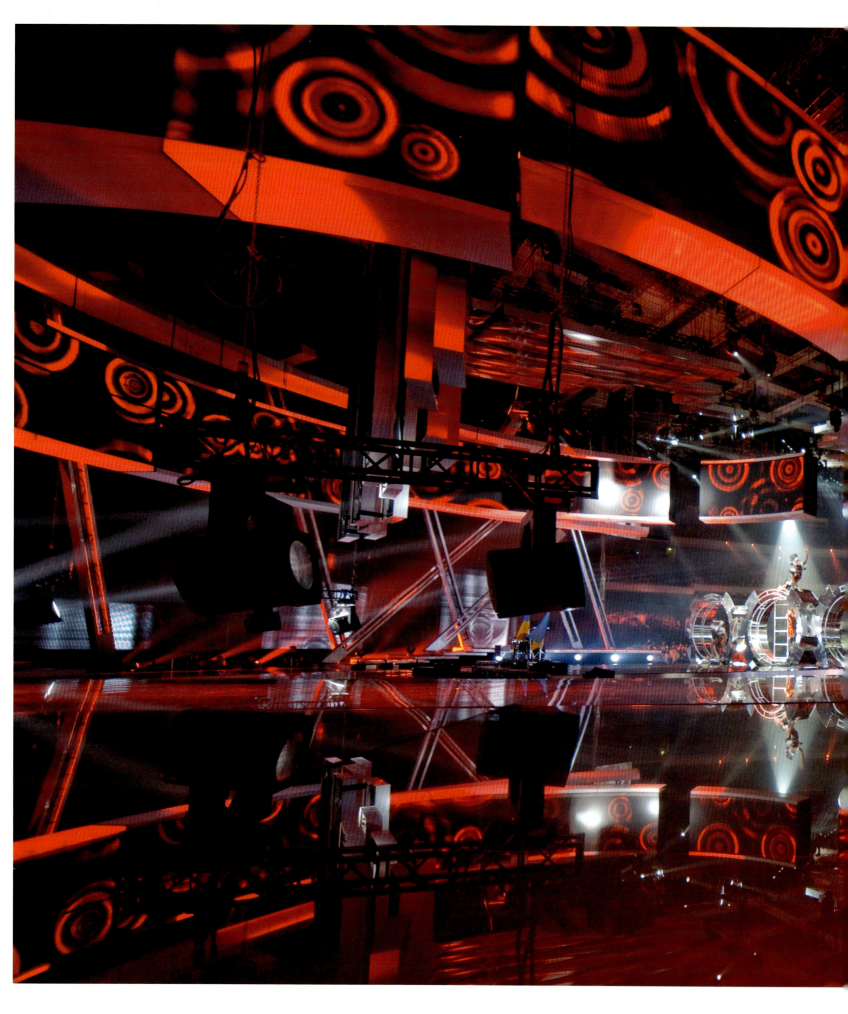

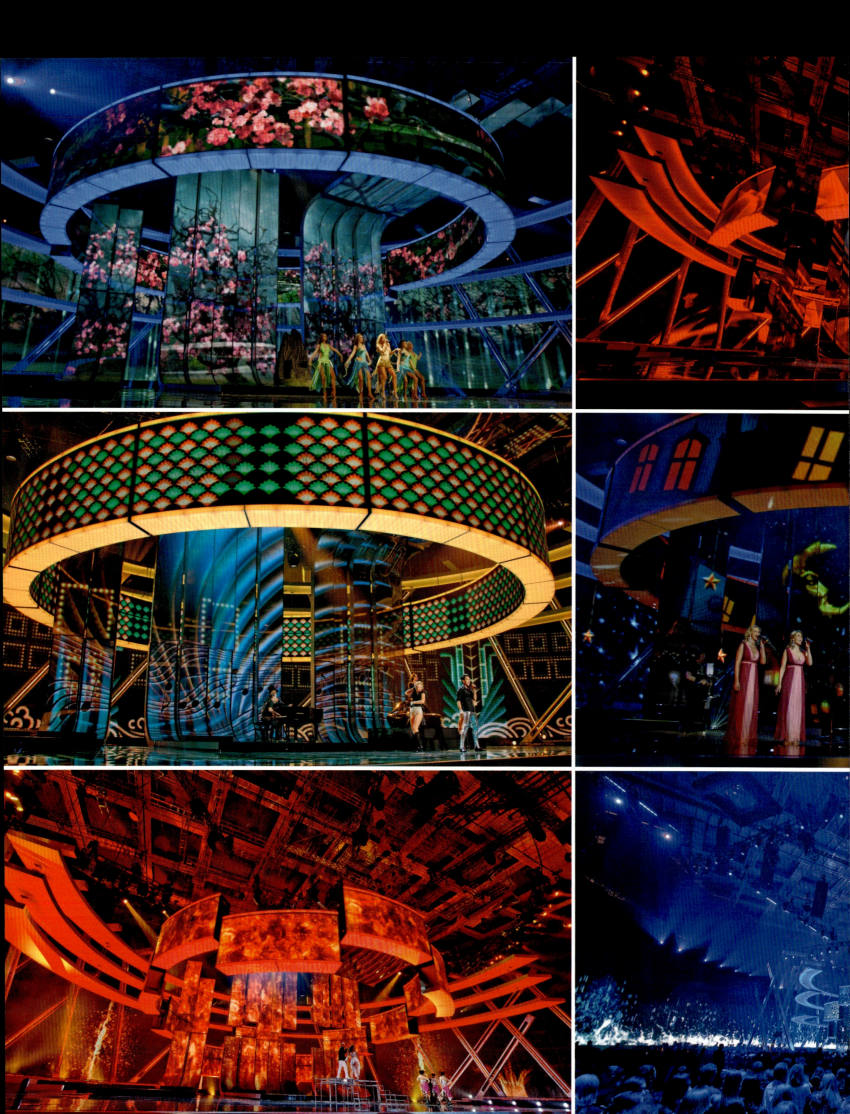

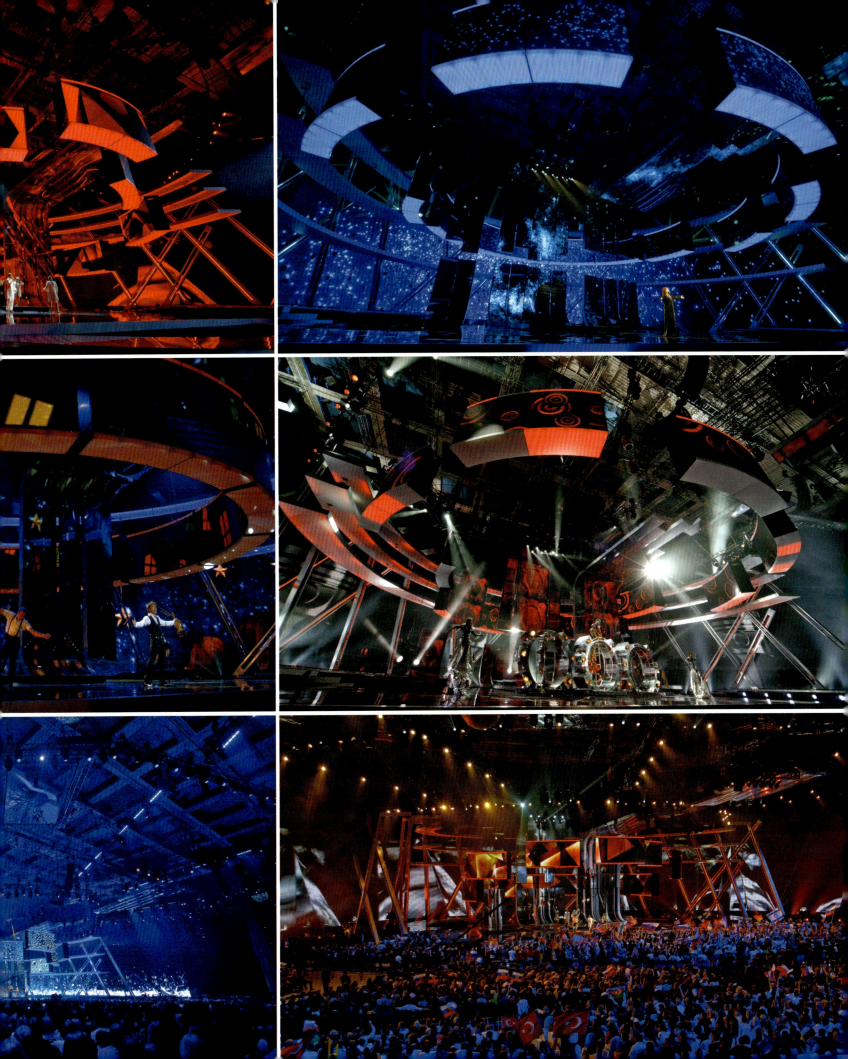

325

SPECIAL EVENT

NOBEL Prize Banquet 2009
City Hall Stockholm
Sweden | 2009

Mercedes-Benz Carwalk, IAA 2007
Festhalle Frankfurt
Germany | 2007

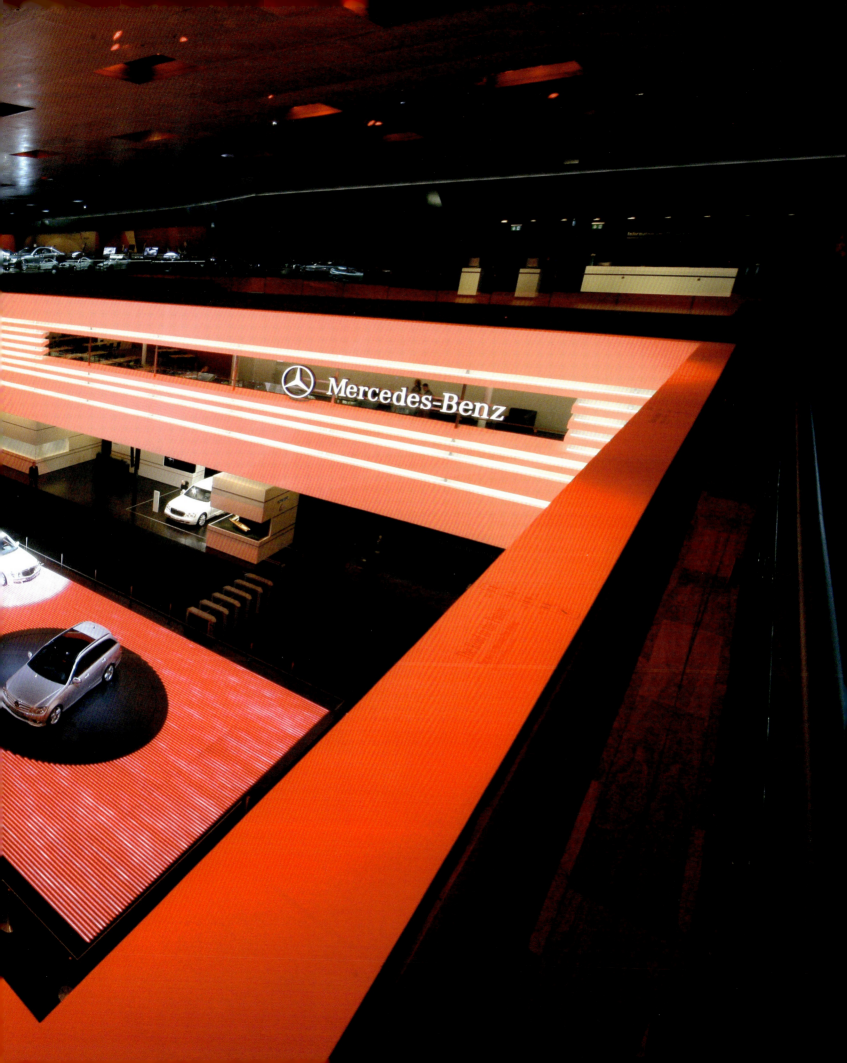

BOSS Black Fashion Show
Fall/Winter Collection 2010
Main Tropical Greenhouse,
Botanic Garden Berlin
Germany | 2009

MAYDAY 2010
Westfalenhallen
Dortmund
Germany | 2010

AIDAdiva – Ship of Light
Hamburg
Germany | 2007

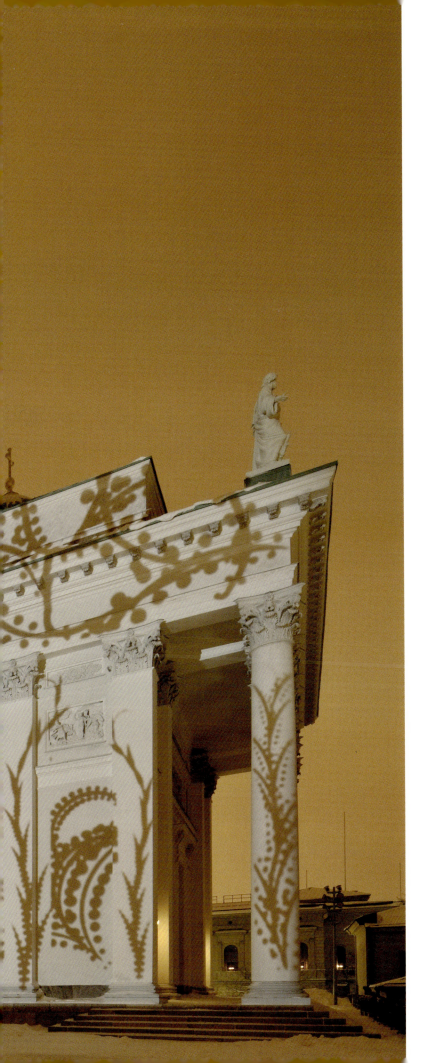

Season of Light 2010
Senate Square & Parliament House Helsinki
Finland | 2010

**BIOGRAFIE/BIOGRAPHY
KÜNSTLERVERZEICHNIS/CREDITS
DANK/ACKNOWLEDGEMENTS**

BIOGRAFIE/BIOGRAPHY

Ralph Larmann, Jahrgang 1963, studierte Schlagzeug mit dem Schwerpunkt Popularmusik am Rotterdams Conservatorium, bevor er sich 1991 überwiegend der Fotografie und dem Journalismus zuwandte. Seit 1992 designt und produziert Ralph Larmann hochwertige Bildbände, Konzertbroschüren und Ausstellungskataloge für Unternehmen und unterschiedlichste Künstler aus der Welt der Rock- und Popmusik sowie der Klassik, seit 2000 mit seinem eigenen Full-Service-Unternehmen, der Ralph Larmann Company. Als freier Fotograf erstellt er für Künstler, Unternehmen, Architekten, Lichtdesigner und Magazine aufwändige Fotodokumentationen auf nationalem und internationalem Parkett. Eine Vielzahl von Stars, Inszenierungen, Events und Produktionen konnte Ralph Larmann seit 1989 in faszinierenden Fotografien festhalten. So produzierte er zuletzt unter anderem für die Band U2 eine aufwändige Fotodokumentation zu einigen Konzerten der 360°-Tournee sowie für David Garrett die Fotos zur DVD „Rock Symphonies Open Air 2010". In seinem Bildband STAGE DESIGN, der im September 2007 in mehr als 120 Ländern erschien, fasste er auf 400 Seiten 30 Produktionen aus den Bereichen Theater, Oper, Musical, Konzerttournee, TV-Show und Special Event visuell im Detail und aus Blickwinkeln zusammen, die dem Zuschauer so meist verschlossen bleiben.

www.larmann.com

Ralph Larmann was born in 1963 and studied drumming at the Rotterdam Conservatorium. During his studies he focused mainly on popular music before deciding to devote himself to photography and journalism in 1991. Since 1992 he has been designing and producing high quality illustrated books, concert brochures and exhibition catalogues for artists and companies from the rock, pop and classical music scenes. In 2000 he started his own comprehensive business service when he founded the Ralph Larmann Company. Working nationally and internationally as a freelance photographer and author, he creates elaborate photo and text documentaries for companies, architects, lighting designers and magazines. Indeed, from as early as 1989 Ralph Larmann has been capturing a great variety of stars and celebrities, productions and events in fascinating photographs and with his recent high quality photo documentation of several U2 tour concerts from their 360° tour and the photos of David Garrett's DVD "Rock Symphonies Open Air 2010" we have the results of two of his most recent creative endeavors. A creativity which we can also see in his illustrated book "STAGE DESIGN", published in September 2007 and distributed in more than 120 countries. In this book Ralph Larmann compiled 400 pages from 30 productions from the theater, the opera, musicals, concert tours, TV shows and special events. The richness of detail, which his photographs show here give us another perspective on and unique access to the fascinating world of the stage.

www.larmann.com

KÜNSTLERVERZEICHNIS/CREDITS

MUSICAL

Wicked – Die Hexen von Oz
Years of Production in Stuttgart: 2007 - 2010
Location: Palladium Theater Stuttgart, Germany
Composer/Lyricist: Stephen Schwartz
Author: Winnie Holzman
Director: Joe Mantello
Associate Director: Lisa Leguillou
Translator Book: Ruth Deny
Translator Lyrics: Michael Kunze
Script Supervisor: Kevin Schröder
Musical Supervisor: Stephen Oremus
Associate Conductor UK: Joel Fram
Choreographer: Wayne Cilento
Dance Supervisor: Mark Myars & Corinne McFadden
Scenic Designer: Eugene Lee
Associate Scenic Designer: Edward Pierce
Assistant Scenic Designer:
Armond "Nick" Francone
Costume Designer: Susan Hilferty
Costume Supervisor: Margie Bailey
Sound Designer: Tony Meola
Associate Sound Designer: Kai Harada
Assistant Sound Designer Intern: Misa Miyabara
Lighting Designer: Kenneth Posner
Associate Lighting Designer: Michael Odam & Karen Spahn
Projection Designer: Elaine McCarthy
Associate Projection Designer: Shawn E. Boyle
Assistant Projection Designer: Matthias Strobel
Projection Programmer: Hillary Knox
Wig Designer: Tom Watson
Associate Wig Designer: Jared Janas
Make-Up Designer: Joe Dulude
Production Supervisor: Thom Widman

West Side Story
Date of Production in Niedernhausen: 28 June 2008
Location:
Rhein-Main-Theater Niedernhausen, Germany
Producer and Impresario: Michael Brenner
Executive Producer: Dagmar Windisch
Director and Choreography reproduced by:
Joey McKneely
Set Design: Paul Gallis
Costume Designer: Renate Schmitzer
Lighting Designer: Peter Halbsgut
Make Up Designer: Hannelore Uhrmacher
Technical Supervision: Andreas Rescheneder, Rainer Frenkel

Ich will Spaß!
Years of Production: 2008 - 2009
Location: Collosseum Theater Essen, Germany
Set Design: Christoph Weyers
Assistant Set Design: Johannes Fischer
Lighting Director: Andy Voller
Assistant Lighting Director & Spotcaller: Matt Daw
MA Operator (konv. & Moving): Chris Hirst
Video Design: Arjen Klerkx
Assistant Videodesign: Coen Bouman
MA & Hippo-Operator (Video): Thomas Giegerich
Technical Supervisior: Martin Siebler (SE)
Production Electrician: Andy Peistrup (SE)

Sorbas
Year of Production: 2009
Location: Freilichtbühne Castle Festival Mecklenburgisches Staatstheater Schwerin, Germany
Director: Peter Dehler
Production Manager:
Peter Meißner/Jörg Bernhardt
Set Design: Olaf Grambow
Lighting Design: Torsten König

CONCERT

U2 – 360°
Years of Production: 2009 - 2011
Location: Olympic Stadium Berlin, Germany & Veltins-Arena Gelsenkirchen, Germany & Wembley Stadium London, UK
Show Designer & Director: Willie Williams
Architect: Mark Fisher
Production Manager: Jake Berry
Kinetic Screen Design: Chuck Hoberman
Screen Concept & Design: Frederic Opsomer
Production & Technical Design: Jeremy Lloyd
Technical Coordinator: Nick Evans
Primary Steelwork Fabrication: Stage Co., Hedwig DeMeyer, Dirk DeDecker
Show Sound Design: Joe O'Herlihy
Video Consultant: Tom Krueger
Video Director: Stefaan Desmedt
Lighting Director: Ethan Weber
Lighting Associate: Alex Murphy
Style Consultant: Sharon Blankson
Show Consultant: Gavin Friday
Choreographer: Morleigh Steinberg
Stage Managers: Rocko Reedy & George Reeves
Sound Crew: Chief Jo Ravitch
Lighting Crew: Chief Nick Barton
Head Rigger: Todd Mauger
Head of Automation: Raff Buono
Structural & Membrane Engineering: Neil Thomas, Atelier One, Luis Fernandez, David Miller, Adelyne Albrecht, Gavin Sayers, David Dexter Associates
Video Screen Design & Engineering: Hoberman Associates, Innovative Designs, Buro Happold, Atelier One, Wi Creations, Barco, Richard Hartman
Performance Stage Fabrication: Tait Towers
Performance Stage Engineering: MG McLaren
Pylon Fabrication: Brilliant Stages
Membrane Fabrication: Architen Landrell
Polyp Mushrooms: Steel Monkey Engineering
Ripple Drums: Specialz Ltd
Automation: Kinesys Projects Ltd
Presentation Animation: Adrian Mudd

Lighting Supplier: PRG
Video Supplier: XL Video
Audio Supplier: Clair
Video Content Production: The Third Company

Kylie Minogue – KYLIEX2008
Years of Production: 2008 - 2009
Location: O2 Arena London, UK
Executive Producers:
Terry Blamey & Kylie Minogue
Created, Directed & Designed by: William Baker
Tour Manager: Sean Fitzpatrick
Production Manager: Kevin Hopgood
Technical Manager: Phil Murphy
Lighting Designers:
Bryan Leitch & Nick Whitehouse
Lighting Crew Chief: Jonathan Sellers
Production Coordinator: Juliette Baldrey
Stage Manager: Toby Plant
Producer: Ten Minutes Touring Company Ltd.
Video Screen Content:
Marcus Viner & Tom Colbourne
Video Director: William Baker & Marcus Viner
FOH Engineer: Chris Pyne
Monitor Engineer: Rod Matheson
Lighting Equipment: Neg Earth Lights
Sound Equipment: Capital Sound Hire Limited
Video Equipment: Blink TV
Set Equipment: Total Fabrications Ltd

The Police – Reunion Tour
Years of Production: 2007 - 2008
Location: American Airlines Center Dallas, USA
Lighting Design: Patrick Woodroffe
Associate Designer/Programmer: Danny Nolan
Assistant Lighting Designer: Adam Bassett
Set Design: Patrick Woodroffe, Charlie Hernandez
Video Content: Danny Nolan/Jim Gable
Production Manager: Charlie Hernandez
Tour Stage Manager: Dug Wiest
Tour Manager: William Francis
Video Director: Kevin Williams

Lighting Equipment:
Upstaging Inc. (USA) & Neg Earth (Europe)
Sound Equipment: Clair Brothers
Video Equipment: Screenworks
Stage Equipment: Tait Towers

Genesis – Turn it on again
Year of Production: 2007
Location: Olympic Stadium Munich, Germany
Set Design: Mark Fisher & Jeremy Lloyd
Architectural Design: Ray Winkler
Visualization: Adrian Mudd & Ric Lipson
Technical Supervisor: Richard Hartman
Lighting Designer: Patrick Woodroffe
Lighting Operator: Dave Hill
Associate Lighting Designer: Adam Bassett
Production Manager:
Steve "Pud" Jones, Howard Hopkins
Production Co-Coordinator: Wob Roberts
Tour Producer: Tony Smith
Coordinator Video equipment:
Bill Lord for Blink TV
FOH Engineer: Michel Colin
Monitor Engineer: Alain Schneebeli
Lighting Equipment: Neg Earth
Sound Equipment: Hyperson
Video Equipment: XL Video
Stage Equipment: StageCo, Brilliant Stages

P!nk – Funhouse
Year of Production: 2009
Location: SAP ARENA Mannheim, Germany
Show Director & Lighting Designer:
Barry "Baz" Halpin
Set Designer: Mark Fisher
Production Manager: Richard Young
Stage Manager: Brian Wares
Lighting Director: Trent O'Connor
Lighting Crew Chief: Roy Hunt
Visuals Designer: Olivier Goulet
Video Consultant: Larn Poland
Video Director: Richard Parkin
FOH Engineer: Chris Madden

Monitor Engineer: Horst Hartman
Lighting Equipment: PRG
Sound Equipment: Concert Sound Clair
Video Equipment: XL Video
Stage Equipment: Brilliant Stages

a-ha – Ending on a High Note
Year of Production: 2010
Location: Sør Arena Kristiansand, Norway
Tour Manager: Kleopatra Tuemmler
Production Manager: James Maillardet
Stage Manager: Tyrone Brunton
Production Assistant: Alice Mather
Show Designer: JoJo Tillmann
FOH Engineer: Sherif El Barbari
Monitor Engineer: Kursten Smith
Sound Crew Chief: Al Woods
Lighting Crew Chief: Andreas "Woody" Wodzinski
Camera Director: Thorsten Hantel
Visual Director: Thomas Krautscheid
Staging Coordinator: Martin Mathisen
StageCo Crew Chief: Stefaan Van Den Bosch
Lighting Equipment: satis&fy AG Werne
Sound Equipment: Capital Sound Hire Ltd.
Video Equipment: Comtech
Stage Equipment: StageCo

DJ Bobo – Fantasy
Years of Production: 2009 - 2010
Location: Lanxess-Arena Cologne, Germany
Creative Team: Dj Bobo, Nancy Baumann, Curtis Burger, Daniel Burkart, Eddy Frühwirth
Producer: Yes Production CH
Artwork: Geoffrey Gillespie
Tour Manager: Stefan Siebert
Production Manager: Eddy Frühwirth
Lighting Designer: Thomas Dietze
Special Effects: Manfred Weniger
Stage Design: Eddy Frühwirth
Sound, Light, Set:
Hico Veranstaltungstechnik GmbH

Die Fantastischen Vier – Fornika für Alle
Year of Production: 2007
Location: Lanxess-Arena Cologne, Germany
Lighting & Set Design:
Gunther Hecker/Gunther Hecker GmbH
Video Content Design:
And.Ypsilon, Kai Reinhardt, Franz Schlechter
FOH Engineer: Klaus Scharff
System Engineer: Johan Schreuder
Sound Technicians:
Stephan Haradz, Joachim Härm
Sound Equipment: satis&fy AG Werne

Bon Jovi – Lost Highway
Years of Production: 2007 - 2008
Location: Commerzbank-Arena Frankfurt, Germany
Set Designer: Doug "Spike" Brant
Video Director: Tony Bongiovi, Anthony Bongiovi
Video Content: Marcia Kapustin & Marcus Lyall
Show Director: Justin Collie
Lighting Director: Pat Brannon
Lighting Operator: Doug "Spike" Brandt
Lighting Crew Chief: Storm Sollars
Sound Equipment: Clair Brothers Audio
Production Manager: John "Bugzee" Hougdahl
Production Coordinator: Jesse Sandler
Head Rigger: Mike Farese
Venue Security Director:
Knute "Mr. Incredible" Brye
Lead site Cooperator: Albert Lawrence
Lighting Equipment:
Ed and Ted's Excellent Lighting
Video Equipment: Nocturne Productions
Stage Equipment: Tait Towers, StageCo

Tina Turner –
Tina!: 50th Anniversary World Tour
Years of Production: 2008 - 2009
Location: SAP ARENA Mannheim, Germany/2009
Production & Set Design: Mark Fisher
Production Manager: Malcolm Weldon
Creative Director/Associate Producer:
Barry "Baz" Halpin

Executive Tour Producer: Roger Davies
Executive Tour Director: Nick Cua
Tour Coordinator:
Bonus Management Inc. & Bill Comstock Buntain
Stage Manager: Seth Goldstein
Set Construction Project Manager: Nick Evans
Video Director: Larn Poland
Musical Direction & Arrangements: Ollie Marland
Video Content Design/Production: Olivier Goulet
FOH Engineer: Dave Natale
Monitor Engineer: Marty Strayer
Lighting Director: Kathy Beer
Lighting Crew Chief: Ian Tucker
Lighting Equipment: PRG Lighting
Sound Equipment: Clair Brothers Audio
Video Equipment: Nocturne Video
Stage Equipment: Tait Towers

Mario Barth Worldrecord Show
Date of Production: 12 July 2008
Location: Olympic Stadium Berlin, Germany
Produced by Hauptstadthelden

OPERA

Aida
Year of Production: 2010
Location: Water Stage Bregenz, Austria
Producer: Bregenzer Festspiele GmbH
Director: Graham Vick
Set Design: Paul Brown
Lighting Design: Wolfgang Göbbel

Tosca
Years of Production: 2007 - 2008
Location: Water Stage Bregenz, Austria
Producer: Bregenzer Festspiele GmbH
Director: Philipp Himmelmann
Set Design: Johannes Leiacker
Lighting Design: Davy Cunningham

Die Passagierin
Year of Production: 2010
Location: Festspielhaus Bregenz, Austria
Producer: Bregenzer Festspiele GmbH
Director: David Pountney
Set Design: Johan Engels
Lighting Design: Fabrice Kebour

Nabucco
Year of Production: 2008
Location: Stade de France Paris, France
Producer: Peter Kroone
Director: Yoel Levi
Project Manager: Marianne Schipper
General Director: Floor Biemans
Stage Manager: Charles Roubaud
Lighting Designer: Fabrice Kebour
Lighting Director: Ralph Schrader
Lighting Project Manager: Peter Oberhofer
Technical Manager: Boris Beplate
Lighting Crew: Ralph Hackstedt, Heiko Sap,
Batu Pamukcuoglu, Markus Damal
Headrigger: Thomas Golücke
Rigger: Rainer List, Jan Kleinenbrands, Oliver Bahn, Mike Elsenplässer

TV SHOW

Eurovision Song Contest 2010
Date of Production: 29 May 2010
Location: Telenor Arena Oslo, Norway
Lighting Designer: Al Gurdon
Lighting Gaffer: Rich Gorrod
Operators:
Andy Voller, Ian Reith, Michael Oz Owen, Theo Cox
Creative/Multicamera Director:
Ole Jørgen Grønlund & Kim Strømstad
Set Designer: Kirsten Weltzin, Bonsak Schieldrop, Trond Olav Erga, Audun Stjern
Production Manager: Ola Melzig
Production Assitant: Joan Lyman Melzig & Cæcilie Hørup Nilsson
Project Manager: Matthias Rau (PRG)
Lighting Crew Chief: Olaf Pötcher (PRG)

Sommer Wetten, dass..?
Date of Production: 23 June 2007
Location: Coliseo Balear Palma de Mallorca, Spain
Director: Frank Hof
Lighting Director: Michael Donecker
Set Design: Pit Fischer
Sound Director: Klaus Wesselsky
Rigging: Team Bremen

Eurovision Song Contest 2009
Date of Production: 16 May 2009
Location: Olimpijski-Arena Moscow, Russia
Lighting Designer: Al Gurdon
Set Designer: John Casey
Production Manager: Ola Melzig
Technical Production Manager: Matthias Rau
Assistant Production Manager: Tobias Åberg
Production Assitant: Joan Lyman Melzig, Olga Morr
Operator: Andy Voller, Ben Cracknell, Ian Reith und Timo Kauristo
Lighting Crew Chief: Frank Karpinski (PRG)

SPECIAL EVENT

NOBEL Prize Banquet 2009
Date of Production: 10 December 2009
Location: City Hall Stockholm, Sweden
Production Manager: Ola Melzig
Project Manager: Mats Andréasson
Lighting Designer: Per Sundin
Lighting Operator: Emma Landare
Production Assistant: Joan Lyman Melzig

Mercedes-Benz Carwalk, IAA 2007
Date of Production: 13 – 23 September 2007
Location: Festhalle Frankfurt, Germany
Auftraggeber: Daimler AG
Architektur: Kaufmann Theilig & Partner Freie Architekten BDA
Kommunikation, Ausstellung und Mediendesign: Atelier Markgraph GmbH
Lichtdesign: TLD Planungsgruppe GmbH
Messebau: Ernst F. Ambrosius & Sohn

BOSS Black Fashion Show Fall/Winter Collection 2010
Date of Production: 28 January 2009
Location: Botanic Garden Berlin, Germany
Producer: Nowadays – Creative Production
Concept: Nowadays – Creative Production
Managing Director: Marcus Kurz
Executive Producer: Volker Scherz
SHOWTEC Project Manager: Frank Vogelsgesang
Lighting Design: Andreas "Woody" Wodzinski
Operator: Oliver Ranft

MAYDAY 2010
Date of Production: 30 April 2010
Location: Westfalenhallen Dortmund, Germany
Client: I-Motion GmbH
Production:
EBS lights Veranstaltungstechnik GmbH
Design and Concept: Mario Kommorofski (EBS), Tobias Weiser (EBS), Marco André Beck (EBS)
Project Manager: Mario Kommorofski (EBS)
Project Manager Assistance: Andreas Schommer (EBS)
Video Content: Matt Finke (Looplight)
Operator Lighting: Benedikt Moser (EBS)
Operator Sound: Tim Ehrenfried (EBS)
Operator Video: Matt Finke (Looplight), Timo Weinhold (Looplight)
CAD: Jan-Philipp Pryss (EBS)
C1 Technic: Jimmy Lange (Cyberhoist/RCL)
Stage Setting: Markus Hofmann (EBS)
LED System: Jens Heubach (curveLED/tennagels)
Laser: Daniel Brune (Laserfabrik)

AIDAdiva – Ship of Light
Date of Production: 20 April 2007
Location: Hamburg, Germany
Art Director: Gert Hof
Management: Asteris Koutoulas
Lighting Equipment:
A&O Lighting Technology, PRG GmbH
Laserfabrik Showlaser GmbH: Daniel Brune
FlashArt (Pyro): Markus Katterle, Sven Asamoa

Operator: Jens Probst
Technical Director: Gerd Helinski
Technical Supplier/Operator: PRG Hamburg
Logistics: Bauer Concept/Norman Bauer

Season of Light 2010
Date of Production: 01 – 06 January 2010
Location: Senate Square & Parliament House Helsinki, Finland
Designer: Mikki Kunttu
Composer: Kasperi Laine
Graphic Content:
Peppe Tannemyr & Lennart Wåhlin
Operator: Mikko Linnavuori
Technical Manager: Jussi Kallioinen

DANK / ACKNOWLEDGEMENT

Ganz herzlichen Dank an die folgenden Menschen, die mich in meiner Arbeit zu STAGE DESIGN EMOTIONS vertrauensvoll unterstützt haben:
Many thanks to the following people who supported me so faithfully during my work on STAGE DESIGN EMOTIONS:
Denis Papin (XL Video Germany),
Bill Lord for Blink TV
Tom Bilsen (StageCo group)
Willie Williams, Mark Fisher, Frances McCahon, Jake Berry,
Ralph-Jörg Wezorke (Lightpower)
Oliver Schlossarek (StageCo Germany GmbH),
Werner Herbst (StageCo Germany GmbH)
Wob Roberts, Patrick Woodroffe
JoJo Tillman, Kleopatra Tuemmler
Eddy Frühwirth (Hico Veranstaltungstechnik)
Gunther Hecker,
Babette Karner, Axel Renner
Ralph Schrader, Peter Oberhofer
Alex Ostermaier (N&M)
Edelgard Marquardt (sennheiser)
Michi Schmitt (Michi Illustrations)
Richard "Richi" Profe, Roland Lambrette, Angela Kratz,
Mikki Kunttu,
Ola Melzig, Joan Lyman Melzig, Per Sundin,
Asteris Koutoulas, Gert Hof, Christine Uckert
Volker Scherz

Tobias Weiser, Marco Beck
Brigitte Schindler (Linguatec Sprachtechnologie)
Hans-Jürgen „Lauti" Lautenfeld (Trend Event)
Uli Steinle (German Light Products GmbH)
Michael Boßmann
Marcus Krömer
Barry „Baz" Halpin
Björn Gaentzsch (Lightpower)
Töne Stallmeyer, Ralf Ehrhardt, Mike Stursberg, Simon Pallasch, Christiane Wolf, Volker Weicker, Ollie Olma
Thilo M. Kramny für sein Vertrauen in meine Arbeit und dieses Projekt!/Thilo M. Kramny for his confidence in my work and this project!
Konstantin Frhr. v. Gaisberg-Schöckingen, Petra Model und Susanne Guidera
Tabea Nagel (Du bist fantastisch/you are fantastic!!!)
Sowie einigen Menschen mehr, die durch ein kleines Zutun etwas Wichtiges für dieses Buch bewegt haben. Vielen Dank!!!/As well as many more people because every bit of their help was so important for this book. Thank you so much!!!

Ein besonderer Dank gilt meiner unglaublich geliebten Christiane (YOU'RE THE ONE), die an einigen Bildern - wie auch dem Cover dieses Buches (UNSER BILD) - maßgeblich beteiligt ist, und meinem Sohn Philipp - You're simply the best!
My special thanks go to my incredibly loved Christiane (YOU'RE THE ONE), who is significantly involved in many of my pictures – as well as the cover of this book ("OUR PICTURE") - and my son Philipp: You're simply the best!